Assembly Stories from Around the World

Heroes of the Faiths

Assembly Stories from Around the World

Heroes of the Faiths

William Dargue

Oxford University Press 1985

Oxford University Press, Walton Street, Oxford OX2 6DP

Oxford New York Toronto
Delhi Bombay Calcutta Madras Karachi
Kuala Lumpur Singapore Hong Kong Tokyo
Nairobi Dar es Salaam Cape Town
Melbourne Auckland

and associated companies in
Beirut Berlin Ibadan Micosia

Oxford is a trade mark of Oxford University Press
© William Dargue 1985
First published 1985

ISBN 0 19 917103 3

Filmset by Christie Typeset (UK) Ltd., Bristol
Printed in Great Britain by Butler & Tanner Ltd., Frome

Contents

The Christians

The Buddhists

The Bodhisattva

Siddhartha Gautama (563-483 BCE) spent many, many lives on earth attaining the spiritual perfection that led him finally to enlightenment. From the time of his meeting with Dipankara, a previous Buddha, in an earlier life, it was certain that he would eventually attain perfection himself. From that time onwards he is referred to as the Bodhisattva. From the date of his enlightenment in 528 BCE he is known as the Buddha. There are probably hundreds of stories told of the Buddha's former lives, some of them even telling of his animal existences, and all of them pointing out features that we might follow in order to eventually achieve our own enlightenment.

Bodhisattva, the merchant's son

Buddhists believe that you do not live just one life, but many. Before the Buddha came to understand the truth and died never to be reborn again, he too had lived many lives. This is a story of the time he was born as the son of a rich Indian merchant.

Many years ago when King Brahmadatta was ruling in Benares the Bodhisattva (the Buddha-to-be) was born as the son of a rich merchant. The merchant trained his son in all the things merchants need to know. He was taught to read and write, to count and to add up; he learnt all about the different things that were bought and sold — silks and carpets, spices and tea, and beautiful things made of metal; and he travelled with the ox-carts and camels that his father led across India and to countries far away.

At last the merchant told Bodhisattva that he was old enough to go on a journey by himself. 500 ox-carts were loaded high with things to sell as well as with wood and water, oil and rice for cooking and tents for sleeping in on the long journey. And they set off.

After Bodhisattva had led the long line of oxen for a week, they came to a great desert. It stretched further than the eye could see and the sun burned down on the dusty sand. After travelling for only an hour the Bodhisattva called the line to halt. The sand was so dry and fine that you couldn't hold it in your fist, and walking on it was like walking on a burning fire. And so, although it was still morning, Bodhisattva told the men to put up their tents and sleep during the day. They would travel in the cool of the night.

Men and oxen slept in the shade of the tents while the sun glared down during the day. As the sun set that evening fires were lit and food was prepared and the men ate their fill before the night's journey. And then the tents were packed away and the great line of oxen set off across the desert once more. They had with them a desert pilot who would normally find the way across the sandy wastes by following the sun. But at night he could recognise the stars and find his way by following their patterns. The desert pilot would lie flat on his back on cushions laid on the front ox-cart so that he could watch the sky and tell the drivers which way to go.

As the rising sun began to light up the sky the line of carts stopped, tents were put up and food was prepared and by the time the desert sand shimmered in the heat, the men and oxen were all safely sleeping in the shade. By day they slept and by night they travelled.

Night after night the desert pilot lay on his back and guided them towards the place where they were to sell their goods. At last they had struggled across nearly 300 km of dry dusty desert and they needed only one more night's journey to come to lands where grass and trees grew and where rivers flowed. This was just as well, because they had hardly any food or water left and no wood at all.

As they packed up their camp that evening for the last night's travel everyone felt happy that they were nearly out of this burning empty place. The desert pilot lay on his back on the soft cushions in the ox-cart and with the tiredness from the long journey and the gentle jogging of the cart through the soft sand, he gradually fell fast asleep. That night the pilot's ox wandered about in the desert wherever he wanted to go, so that by morning the line of oxen arrived back at the last place they had camped.

'Stop!' called the pilot. 'We've come the wrong way. I must have fallen asleep.'

'We've run out of food and water,' grumbled the drivers, 'and we've no wood either. We're all going to die in the desert.'

The Bodhisattva looked around and noticed one or two tiny tufts of desert grass growing nearby. 'If grass can grow here,' he said, 'there must be water somewhere.' And Bodhisattva took a spade and began to dig.

Soon the other men joined in the digging and the hole got deeper. From time to time as the hot sun rose higher in the sky and the men grew thirsty and tired there were moanings and grumblings. But Bodhisattva worked steadily knowing that grass needs water to survive, so there must be water somewhere.

After midday when the sun was high in the sky and was at its hottest the diggers struck an enormous rock at the bottom of the hole. They were already over 30m deep, as deep as a house, and the men threw down their spades and wept in despair.

Bodhisattva put his ear to the rock and faintly he could hear the movement of water beneath. 'We must not give up,' he said. 'If we keep trying we might die looking, but we might find water. If we give up we will surely die.'

The Bodhisattva called to his page boy to bring an iron hammer and told him to hit the rock as hard as he could. As the boy hit the rock a small crack appeared across the middle. As everyone watched the split grew bigger and bigger and water began to seep through. Then a great fountain of water burst out and soaked everyone standing by. They all scrambled to get out of the hole which was quickly filling up with bubbling water.

There were shouts of joy all round as men and animals drank the refreshing water. As the sun set that night the ox-carts followed the desert pilot who led them out of the sandy wasteland to the green pastures beyond.

*

Before he became the Buddha and fully understood how human beings might be saved, the Bodhisattva had already made his promise:

However many millions of living beings there are,
   I promise to save them all.
However many sins there are,
   I promise to give them all up.
However difficult the laws are,
   I promise to understand them.
However hard it is to understand the truth,
   I promise that I will understand it.

(*from* The Bodhisattva's Vow)

*

Prince Dighavu

Many Buddhist stories are set in the time of King Brahmadatta of Benares (modern Varanasi, Uttar Pradesh, India). It seems likely that such a king existed although it is impossible to pinpoint his reign with any accuracy and the custom of setting a story in the reign of Brahmadatta equates with the traditional 'once upon a time' of English story-telling. Nothing is known of Prince Dighavu than is told here and the story serves to indicate the importance of one of the main tenets of Buddhist philosophy ie. that the only way to overcome hatred is by loving-kindness, that hatred serves no purpose in human society nor in the progress of the individual towards his own salvation.

*

Prince Dighavu

In the north of India is the great city of Benares. Many years ago it was the capital city of King Brahmadatta's cruel empire. King Brahmadatta was a rich and powerful king who enjoyed ruling over his own people and was always on the look-out for other lands to conquer.

Not far from Benares was the small country of Kosala ruled by the kind and gentle King Dighiti. King Dighiti did not have much of an army for he was not at all like Brahamadatta. Dighiti believed in the words of the Buddha that hatred can never be beaten by hatred, only by love. King Brahmadatta would have laughed if he had heard these words, and he prepared his army to attack the tiny kingdom of Kosala.

In a matter of days King Dighiti's happy little kingdom was turned into a land of suffering and pain. King Brahmadatta's soldiers swept through the countryside with their troops of elephants and horses, with their bows and spears and swords and attacked the capital city. King Dighiti managed to escape into hiding with his wife.

The years passed and King Dighiti and his queen came to live in a poor hut outside the city of Benares. Things were hard for the King and Queen, for they had no money and no way of earning any, and they had a baby boy to look after, their son Prince Dighavu. But whenever the Queen got angry at the thought of King Brahmadatta living in luxury in his palace while they starved, King Dighiti always reminded her that you can't get rid of hate by hating, only love and kindness can conquer hate. Whenever their son as he grew up threatened to get revenge on the evil Brahamadatta, the good King Dighiti always said the same thing.

The Prince Dighavu grew older and King Dighiti sent him to a friendly king of another country to be educated in safety away from the cruel Brahmadatta. And as he said goodbye to his son King Dighiti reminded him that hate could never conquer hate, only loving-kindness could conquer hate.

It was while Prince Dighavu was coming back home after many years away that his father and mother were found by King Brahmadatta. Dighiti's old barber spotted him in the streets of Benares and was given a reward by the King for telling him. Brahmadatta's soldiers arrived to arrest the old King and Queen and led them away. And so it was that the first time Prince Dighavu had seen his parents for many years, they were being dragged in chains to Brahmadatta's prison to be executed. Dighavu rushed up to his parents with tears in his eyes and cried out angrily, 'I shall have my revenge on the wicked Brahmadatta. He shall not treat you like this and get away with it.'

But his father calmly told him: 'You will never conquer hate by hating; only love will conquer hatred.'

Later that day the old King and Queen were executed, but the same night Prince Dighavu managed to get the prison guards drunk and smuggle out his parents' bodies so that he could hold a proper funeral for them. This worried King Brahmadatta. If Dighiti's son was brave enough to try that he might well be brave enough to get his revenge.

Prince Dighavu found himself a job. It was one of the worst of jobs, working in the King's elephant stables feeding and cleaning out the royal elephants, but it earned him a wage. After a long day's work Dighavu used to sit outside the stables and play and sing. King Brahmadatta heard the singing and sent a servant to find out who could play and sing so well. When he found out that it was the new stable boy who had also shown himself to be honest and clever even at his humble job, King Brahmadatta gave him a much better job in the royal court. Dighavu became one of the courtiers who were with the King everywhere he went. Indeed he did his job so well that very soon the King trusted him in all things.

One day the royal court went out hunting. With the King went many nobles, lords and many courtiers too. It was a wonderful sight to see the great procession of horses and riders with the hunting dogs running along beside. They chased across open country and through woods, over streams and by rivers, over hills and along the valleys, until the night began to draw near. It was then that King Brahmadatta lost his way and soon could not find the rest of the hunt. It was Prince Dighavu who first noticed he was missing.

When Dighavu eventually found the King it was nearly dark. Brahmadatta had tied his horse to a tree and had fallen asleep there. But as he slept he groaned and rolled about. Sometimes he called out in fear. It was clear that the King was having a bad dream.

Dighavu thought to himself, 'The King is having a bad dream because he has a bad conscience. He has done so many wicked things in his life, no wonder he cannot sleep peacefully. Now I am able to forgive Brahmadatta for killing my parents, but if he ever finds out who I really am, he will surely kill me.'

Dighavu drew his sword, but as he did so he remembered his father's words: 'Hate can never be conquered by hate, only by love can hate be conquered.' At that moment King Brahmadatta woke up.

'I am Prince Dighavu,' said the young man, 'the son of King Dighiti and his Queen.'

'Forgive me, Dighavu,' begged the King nervously. 'Grant me my life.'

Dighavu pushed his sword back into its sheath. 'I do not want to take your life,' he said. 'It is you who want to kill me. Grant me my life.' Dighavu explained to the King what his father had taught him, saying that even as he went to his death King Dighiti had told him not to want revenge.

King Brahmadatta had tears in his eyes as he realised what a brave and good man the prince was. He took his hand and swore that they should be friends for ever. And so they were. When they returned to the city of Benares Brahmadatta gave Dighavu his own kingdom back and he gave him his own daughter to be his queen.

*

There is a story told of one of Buddha's earlier lives. He was cruelly attacked by an angry king with a sword and eventually died after the king had cut off his limbs. The Buddha realised that it was no use trying to talk kindly to the king whose mind was blinded with hate and anger, so he patiently put up with his suffering until it was over. And Buddha felt sorrier for the king than he did for himself.

When the Buddha saw his wounds he seemed to feel no pain for his mind was strong, patient and unbroken. What did upset him was to see the king so full of hate and following the path of wickedness. People of real understanding, whose minds are full of love for other people, they don't worry about the things that happen to them; they worry about the things that happen to other people.

(*from* Jatakamala 28 *by Aryasura*)

*

The Buddha

Siddhartha Gautama was born in 563 BCE heir-apparent to a small but prosperous Indian kingdom whose capital lay in the Himalayan foothills. Kapilavastu is about 150 km from Katmandu in modern Nepal. The prince found no comfort in his luxurious surroundings and no solace in the ascetism practised by the Hindu holy men.

After a period of intense meditation he was able to look back over his previous innumerable lives and understand the process that led to his enlightenment. At this point he could have accepted nirvana, the ultimate object of every Buddhist, the extinction of self, but because of his compassion for mankind he chose to preach his message to all people which he did from the age of thirty five until he died at the age of eighty. He spent his life travelling about the north of India teaching and setting up communities of monks wherever he went. A number of stories are told of the Buddha's childhood which point to the fact that he was to be an extraordinary person with an understanding far deeper and a love for living things greater than that of anyone. The stories of his dealings with both the great and the humble are told to point morals and demonstrate quoted lines of his teaching.

The Buddha and the injured swan

There were many signs when the Buddha was young that he was not an ordinary child. When he was born as Prince Siddhartha, a holy man told his father the King that his son would either grow up to be a famous emperor or a great religious teacher. King Suddhodana wanted him to be a great emperor and trained him well in all the things that princes should know.

But one day in early spring the King began to wonder. It was the custom in that land for the King to hold a special ceremony in spring. The Kings and all his court would go out into the fields of the countryside and there the King would help to plough the first furrow. By doing this it was believed that the King would make the crops grow well that year.

The King with all his courtiers in their finest clothes went in procession out into the countryside. There a special golden plough with a team of fine horses was waiting for the King. The lords of the court had their own ploughs and horses too. With a great blowing of trumpets, and cheers from the people watching, the King slowly drove his horses forward and dug the earth ready for the seeds to be sown. Solemnly the lords followed.

Prince Siddhartha was sitting at the edge of the field watching all this. But he did not notice the King in all his rich clothes with his team of strong horses easily pulling the sharp golden plough, and he did not watch the noble lords with their strong oxen waving to the crowds as they followed behind. Siddhartha only noticed the poor farm workers, the people who worked this land every day. He watched as they ran about the field in front of the royal procession, sweating and groaning as they moved the heavy stones that might get in the way of the plough. He saw the horses and the oxen straining to pull along the great weights behind them. And in other fields he saw people ploughing their fields without the help of horses or oxen. Whether the crops grew well or badly that year Prince Siddhartha and the King would never grow hungry. This was not true for the poor farm workers.

Siddhartha sat underneath an apple tree and watched all this. And gradually his mind was completely concentrated on the truth that he had understood, so that when the King's servants came for him, they thought that he had fallen asleep sitting there, and had a job to wake him up. The King was worried when he heard the tale.

The next spring King Suddhodana was told another story about his son, Prince Siddhartha, that made him realise that he would never make a mighty emperor. Little could he know that his son was to be a religious leader followed by millions of people throughout the world.

As the weather grew warmer many wild birds began to fly back to their homes. It was a great time for the hunters. As the flocks of ducks and geese flew across the pale spring sky, the men had plenty to shoot at.

One day a flock of wild swans flapped slowly and gracefully over the palace gardens. They were on their way from the hot lands of the south of India to the north where the lakes of the Himalaya mountains were now unfrozen. As Prince Siddhartha watched the beautiful birds winging their way home an arrow shot up from somewhere nearby and hit the leader of one of the flocks. As the injured bird began to fall to the ground a cheer went up from not far away. Prince Siddhartha recognised one of the voices as that of his cousin, Devadatta.

Full of fear for the bird's life Siddhartha rushed through the gardens to the place where the swan was falling. And when he reached it he gently pulled out the arrow and took the great white bird in his arms to look after it.

Siddhartha took it back to the palace and put ointment on the wound. For the next few days he kept the bird in safety, keeping the wound clean and the bird well fed. When he thought the swan was a little better he set it free to swim on the palace lake until it should be strong enough to fly away to the lakes of the Himalayas and join the rest of the flock.

But news of what Siddhartha had done reached the ears of his cousin, Devadatta. Devadatta sent a messenger to Siddhartha and demanded that the swan be given back to him. After all he had been the one to shoot the bird. Prince Siddhartha sent a message back, 'You did not *kill* the bird,' he said, 'only its flight. I will not give it to you.'

Devadatta was angry when he heard this reply and sent further messages ordering his cousin to let him have what was his.

King Suddhodana soon came to hear of the argument. He did not want it to become a family quarrel and ordered that a jury of his wise men should listen to what both Devadatta and Siddhartha had to say, and then decide who should have the swan.

The day came for the wise men to meet. Devadatta argued that he had been the one to shoot the swan and so it was clear that the bird should be his. But Siddhartha answered, 'My cousin Devadatta tried to take away the swan's life. I healed it and gave it back its life, and so the swan should belong to me.'

The wise men argued and argued. It seemed right that Devadatta should have the bird back. If he *had* killed it it would clearly have belonged to him. But others said that Siddhartha should keep it because he had cared for it. At length the oldest of the wise men spoke up: 'Devadatta tried to take away the swan's life and he failed. Siddhartha gave the swan life by healing it and looking after it. Even the gods cannot give back life once it is taken away. I believe the swan should be given to Siddhartha.'

And so it was. Devadatta held a grudge for many years against this cousin, but this was not the last time that the Prince showed his kindness towards living things.

*

If you want to find everlasting peace, you must help the poor and the ill, you must have a calm mind and you must show loving kindness to all living things. By doing this the wise person will have no sorrow and will find peace.
(*from* the Itivuttaka 22)

*

If you understand peace, your hearts will be full of loving kindness. If you understand that you are no different from everybody else, then you will be ready to help other people. And if you succeed in helping other people you will find Me, and by finding Me you will yourself become Buddha.
(*from* the Hundred Thousand Songs *by Jetsun-Milarepa*)

*

The Buddha and King Pasenadi the Fat

King Pasenadi of Kosala lived at the same time as the Buddha. He respected the Buddha and knew what a great teacher he was, but he was never able to stay awake long enough to hear what the Buddha tried to teach him. The reason was simple: King Pasenadi ate too much.

King Pasenadi ate buckets of rice and curry sauce at every meal time and he never did any exercise apart from sitting on his throne. So when the Buddha came in the evening to teach the King how to find calmness in his soul, the King was so full and tired that he just couldn't concentrate on anything the great teacher said.

'I call my way the Middle Way,' said Buddha. 'You should not starve yourself trying to find the truth, but you shouldn't eat so much that you can't think either.'

Buddha taught these words to the King's nephew:

If you think what you are doing,
if you don't eat too much,
you will not suffer,
but grow old slowly.
(*from the* Dhammapada-attha-katha *by Buddhaghosa 15: 265*)

Buddha told the nephew to say this to the King just before he ate his last mouthful of rice at every meal. The King would not be able to eat this last mouthful when he heard these words and would put it down. The nephew should then order the royal cooks to prepare one mouthful less the next day.

The nephew did this and it was as the Buddha had said. Just as he was about to eat his last mouthful of rice the King heard his nephew reciting the words of the Buddha telling him to east sensible amounts if he wanted to live a long and happy life. He put his food down and declared that he would give a thousand gold coins to the poor people of the city.

The next day the King was given a little less food and his royal nephew said the Buddha's words just as he was about to finish his meal. The same thing happened.

And so day by day, the King gave away thousands of gold coins to the poor people and each day he himself ate a little less food. A time came when the King spent much of his time helping people who did not have enough to eat instead of worrying about how much he had to eat. And the King himself ate only a cup of rice a day. He was much slimmer and very much happier, as the Buddha had said he would be.

The Buddha and the hungry man

There was great excitement in the small town of Alavi in northern India. The Buddha had arrived that morning with his monks with their shaven heads and yellow robes. They were camped in a clearing in the forest just outside the town and everyone was busy about something. All the usual jobs were forgotten and people were getting ready to go and hear the Buddha teach or preparing food for the holy man and his monks to eat.

But for one poor farmer nothing was going right that day. He too wanted to go and meet the famous teacher and was about to set off with the rest of the people from the town to the clearing in the forest. But suddenly his only cow had broken free from its rope and run off into the forest. If he lost that cow, he would lose everying. The poor farmer immediately gave chase. Into the forest he rushed following the footprints left by the animal and worrying all the time that he would not be able to find it or that some wild beast might make a meal of it before he managed to get there.

Eventually he caught up with the cow who was standing quietly chewing the grass in the depths of the forest. He was too tired to be angry, but as he trudged back towards his house he couldn't help thinking of all the other townspeople who were at that very moment listening to the Buddha's teaching. He was missing his only chance to hear what this great man had to say.

It was late when he arrived home tired and hungry. He tied the cow up safely again and decided that if he stayed to eat, he would miss any chance of hearing anything at all. So hungry though he was he went straight away to the clearing in the forest where the Buddha was.

But when he got there, he was surprised to find that the Buddha hadn't even started. All the people were gathered there ready for him to begin, but Buddha sat quietly as if waiting for something. As soon as Buddha saw the poor farmer, hungry and tired, he stood up and welcomed him with a friendly smile. 'Do we have any food left?' he said. 'Bring it for this hungry man and then we can begin.'

The hungry man was surprised but very grateful and gladly ate the food that was brought. But as he finished he could hear some of the monks grumbling and muttering. 'We've had to wait all this time for one poor farmer who couldn't be bothered to turn up on time! And now we have to wait while he eats.'

But the Buddha stood up and spoke to them. 'I know more things than you know,' he said. 'This man has had to work far harder than you to get here to listen to my words. That is why I waited for him. And now he must eat, for no-one can concentrate on what I am about to say if he is worrying about how hungry he is. But now he is here and now he is fed and comfortable I shall begin.'

*

The following words were written by a Chinese buddhist over a thousand years ago:

Don't let everyday things weigh you down, but never try to forget all about them. Only by doing this will you ever become free.

*

You must try really hard all the time. Throughout your life you can never be sure that you will live long enough to take another breath.
(*from the writings of Huang Po*)

*

Queen Samavati

The two wives of King Udena were called Samavati and Magandiya. Every day Queen Samavati sent her servant, Khujjuttara with eight gold coins to buy flowers for the royal palace. Every day Khujjuttara went to a nearby gardener. She put four of the gold coins into her own purse and asked the gardener to give her flowers for the other four coins.

But one day when Khujjuttara called at the gardener's house there was a visitor. It was the Buddha who had been invited for a meal with the gardener. They had eaten and Buddha was talking to the people gathered there about telling lies and being dishonest and how it actually harmed you more than the people you cheated. The servant girl realised the truth of the Buddha's words and that day she spent all eight gold coins on flowers and, of course, came back to the palace with twice as many as ever she had before.

Queen Samavati was surprised when she saw Khujjuttara with a great armful of flowers. 'How have you got so many?' asked the Queen. 'Are the flowers half price today?' The servant remembered the words of the Buddha and she had to tell the truth. When she told the Queen that she had been cheating and lying to her, instead of being angry, Samavati was pleased that she had been brave enough to change her ways and be honest and truthful. Queen Samavati asked Khujjuttara to tell her everything she had heard the Buddha say at the gardener's house. And when the girl had finished she called all her ladies to her and Khujjuttara had to tell the tale again.

After this Queen Samavati sent the servant not only to buy flowers for the palace every day but also to listen to the teaching of Buddha whenever she could. Khujjuttara would come back and tell the Queen and all the ladies what she had heard. And although they had never met the Buddha they all became faithful followers of his.

The Queen was not allowed out of the palace without a great procession of soldiers, but it was her greatest wish to see the Buddha for herself. With a great deal of trouble she and the ladies of the palace knocked a hole in the wall of their room so that they could see out on to the street. If the Buddha happened to pass that way the Queen would be able to at least see him through the hole and throw flower petals in his honour.

But the King's other wife, Queen Magandiya was becoming more and more annoyed at all these carryings-on. She was perhaps jealous that nobody was paying her much attention any more. So she reported to the King that Samavati was planning to murder him, and she took him to see the hole in the Queen's room overlooking the street. 'Samavati planned to kill you as you passed along the street,' said Magandiya, 'otherwise why should she make a secret hole in the wall?'

But Samavati told the King the truth and Udena believed her. Indeed he had his workmen build proper windows into the wall so that Queen Samavati could get a proper view of the Buddha if he came that way.

Magandiya was filled with hatred not only for Samavati but also for the Buddha himself. Secretly she paid a gang of thugs to follow the Buddha and his friends round the town, shouting rude things at them and throwing things.

It became so difficult for the Buddha and his monks that Buddha's faithful friend Ananda said that they ought to leave that city. 'But where would we go, Ananda?' asked Buddha.

'To another city,' Ananda replied.

'And what if the people there shouted rude remarks and threw stones?'

'We'd go somewhere else,' said Ananda.

'And if things were difficult there? Ananda you cannot run away from difficulties. You must stay and face them. Things will be hard but they will get better.'

And so it was. After a week the gang of thugs got fed up of following the monks round the streets and left them alone.

Queen Magandiya had to think of another plan. She sent eight live chickens to the King as a present and suggested to him that Samavati might like to cook them for him. King Udena agreed and asked Samavati to cook the chickens. Samavati had to refuse. As a Buddhist she had promised never to kill any living being. She could not eat meat; she certainly could not kill an animal. But the King did not mind.

Magandiya then had eight dead chickens sent to the King to be given the Buddha and his monks. Again she suggested to the King that he ask Samavati to cook them. This time she agreed: 'As they are dead already I *can* cook them, though whether the Buddha will eat them I do not know.'

'See!' shouted Magandiya. 'She will cook for a penniless monk who wanders about the country like a beggar. And yet she will not cook for her husband the King. My Lord, she cares more about this monk than she cares about you.'

But the King refused to pay any attention to Magandiya's jealousy.

Some days later Magandiya hid a poisonous snake inside the King's lute. She sneaked the instrument into Samavati's room and lay it there with a bunch of flowers across the hole to stop the snake getting out. Later when the King came in from hunting, he went to see Samavati. The snake pushed past the bunch of flowers and began to slither out of the lute. King Udena quickly took his bow and fitted an arrow with which he killed the snake. But in his fright and anger he turned and fired his second arrow at Queen Samavati. And though he had a deadly aim and though the arrow was pointing straight at the Queen's heart, it missed! It was said afterwards that it was her love for the King that protected her.

King Udena was so impressed by Queen Samavati's behaviour despite all the difficulties that his other wife, Magandiya had put in her way, that he too became a follower of the Buddha.

*

The Buddha said:

If you remember how people treated you badly,
how they hit you or beat you or robbed you,
if you remember these things you will live in hate.

If you forget that people treated you badly,
that they hit you or beat you or robbed you,
if you forget these things you will live in love.

Hate never gets rid of hate;

only love can get rid of hate.
(*from the* Dhammapada 3-5)

*

Buddha and the two kings

In the north of India there were two countries next to each other. The frontier between them was a large river for which both peoples were thankful for not only could they travel along the river by boat, and catch fish in it, it always gave them plenty of water for their fields and for themselves during the hot dry summers. So the two countries lived in peace with each other for the river gave them enough water to grow food for all the people.

One summer the weather was particularly hot and no rain fell. But the people who lived near the river ran the water along canals to keep their crops alive and healthy. But as the heat went on the river began to get smaller until at last there was only a small trickle running along the dry river bed.

It happened that two farmers came down one day to this small trickle of water and began to argue as to whose land it should water. They were so angry that they both went back to their farms to get help. Soon there was a large crowd of angry people on each side of the river.

It was not long before this happened in other places along the river and the news came to the two kings.

Emergency messages went out across both lands and soldiers on foot and on horseback were called to arms. Within days two armies were lined up one on each side of the river and the two kings stared at each other across the tiny trickle of water, ready for battle.

This news came to ears of the Buddha who set out as soon as he heard it. He travelled without stopping until he came near to where the two armies were lined up. Buddha camped with his monks a little way from the two armies and then sent one of his monks with a message to the two kings. Buddha asked to see them both immediately.

The two kings knew how wise the Buddha was and came to him straight away. The kings sat down with their government ministers and listened to Buddha. 'Which is most valuable,' he asked, 'the water flowing in the river over there, or the blood flowing in the veins of your people?'

'It is obvious,' said the kings. 'The blood of our people is worth far more than the water of the river.'

'The blood of your people is certainly far more valuable than water,' said Buddha. 'And yet you are both prepared to have the blood of your people spilled in battle for a trickle of water! And what a waste, for there will not be any more water in the river!'

The kings and their people looked away shamefaced.

The Buddha did not need to say anything else. The kings sat together with their ministers and agreed how they should share the small amount of water left in the river. And this was done peacefully.

It was a hard time during the next weeks for the river grew still smaller and many of the fields began to look dry and burned. But there were no more arguments and all the people got their fair share of what water there was.

At last the rains came and there was plenty of water for everyone and the two kings and their people continued to live in peace next to each other.

*

Just a single word that brings peace
  is better than a thousand useless words.
Just a single verse that brings peace
  is better than a thousand useless verses.
Just a single poem that brings peace
  is better than a thousand useless poems.
If a man in battle beats a thousand men
  and then a thousand more,
he is not nearly so great as the man who learns
  to control his own mind.
(*from the* Dhammapada 100-104)

*

The Buddha and Kisa Gotami

There lived in India a poor orphan girl called Kisa Gotami who married a rich young man. The two were very happy together and they were overjoyed when Kisa Gotami gave birth to her first child. It was a boy and they both loved him dearly. It seemed to Kisa that she must be the luckiest person in the world. Her parents had died when she was very young and she had lived a life with so little money that she never knew if she would get anything to eat each day. And now she was married to a rich husband who cared for her and she had a baby son of her own.

But money cannot buy health. It happened that before he had even learned to say his first word, the baby caught a fever and died.

Kisa Gotami was so upset that she rushed out into the street with the dead baby in her arms. She knocked on a neighbour's door and asked if they had any medicine that could cure death. The neighbours shook their heads and smiled sadly. 'I'm afraid we can't help you,' they said.

Kisa Gotami ran from door to door asking the same question of everyone who answered: 'Do you have a medicine that will cure death?'

'I'm sorry,' they all said, 'but we cannot help you.'

As Kisa desperately ran through the streets of the town asking anyone she met she came across a holy man. He had the shaven head and yellow robe of a Buddhist monk. He was carrying his bowl and begging for food.

'Do you know of a medicine that can cure my dead baby?' Kisa asked the monk.

'I cannot do anything to help your baby,' answered the monk, 'but I do know someone who can help *you*. It is the Buddha.'

The monk told Kisa where to find the Buddha who was staying not far away, and there Kisa ran still carrying the body of her child. The Buddha was resting in a clearing in the forest nearby, but Kisa was in such a state of panic that she pushed past the monks who tried to stop her and woke the sleeping Buddha. 'My Lord Buddha,' said Kisa weeping, 'I am told that you can help me. My baby has died and nowhere can I find a medicine to cure him.'

'If you can fetch me a handful of mustard seeds from a house where no-one in the family has died, then I can make a medicine to cure your baby of death.'

So off went Kisa Gotami again round the town, this time asking if anyone could give her a handful of mustard seeds so that the Buddha could make a medicine to cure her dead child. Almost everyone had some mustard seeds to offer her, but when she asked if anyone from the house had ever died, they answered perhaps that their father was dead, or their mother or grandparents. 'The dead are many and the living are few,' they told Kisa, 'Do not remind us of our sorrow.'

And as darkness came and the people of the town began to light their lights in the houses, Kisa sat down tired and weary by the side of the road. At every house she had been to someone in the family had died.

Kisa watched the lights burn in the houses and later in the evening she saw them being blown out. 'How silly I have been,' she thought, 'Of course, all living things must die and there is nothing we can do about it.'

The next day Kisa Gotami buried her baby and went back to the Buddha in the clearing in the forest. This time she spoke calmly to him and told him what she had understood. Buddha said to her, 'You will not find peace in your mind by weeping and wishing for things that cannot be. You must learn that sorrow is like an arrow that has wounded you. You must pull the arrow out before you can be healed.'

Kisa Gotami became a follower of the Buddha.

*

Buddha always taught that it is no use trying to hold on to the things in this life, because everything changes and eventually dies. By following the Buddha's teaching you can find a peace that is nothing to do with this life that will never change. Over 900 years ago the great Tibetan poet Milarepa wrote about things that seem big and strong and precious and how they change and die:

A painting in gold,
flowers of turquoise blue,
a rushing stream in the valley above,
rice growing in the valley below,
great bundles of silk,
a valuable jewel,
the new moon,
a precious child.

But the gold painting begins to fade
   as soon as it is finished;
and soon the beautiful blue flowers will
   be killed by the frost;
the stream rushes powerfully down the high valley
   but it is weak and tame in the valley below;
the rice growing in the valley is soon cut down;
and the wonderful silk cloth is cut with a knife;
someone else will soon own the jewel that
   you love so much;
and the pale moonbeams will fade and disappear;
even the precious child that is born will grow up,
   leave home and go away.

So follow the Buddha's way now.
If you think you can leave it till tomorrow
you will suddenly find that life has slipped away.
Follow the Buddha's way now.

(*from* Milarepa's Song of Transcience with Eight Similes, from the Mila Grubum 20, the Hundred Thousand Songs)

*

How Robber Finger-Necklace became a monk

The Buddha travelled all over India teaching people that they should try to find peace and calm in their minds. He came one day to the land of Kosala in northern India and stayed at the city of Savatthi. Each day he got up and went out into the city to beg silently for food as Buddhist monks still do today. And each day he returned to the place where he was staying to eat. After tidying up the house he would preach to the people of the city who had come to hear him.

One day the Buddha left the house and set off along a small road leading out of the city. He wore his yellow monk's robe and carried with him only his begging bowl. He passed through open countryside where the fields looked uncared for and soon came to a poor village where the houses looked broken and the people thin and afraid.

A man came up to him but put nothing in the Buddha's begging bowl. 'You cannot go along that road,' said the man looking worried. 'Surely you have heard about the danger there.'

'Oh, I'm sure I'll be alright,' answered Buddha. 'I have faced many dangers before.'

'But haven't you heard that Robber Finger-Necklace lives down that road? No-one ever goes that way and comes back alive.'

'Robber Finger-Necklace!' said the Buddha. 'How did he come to have such a strange name?'

The people of the village had gathered round the Buddha by now and a woman stepped forward to explain: 'Robber Finger-Necklace is the cruellest of men,' she said. 'He has no kindness in him whatever. He doesn't just steal from people, he kills them and burns their villages too. He is called Finger-Necklace, because of all the people he murders he cuts off their fingers and hangs them on a necklace around his neck.'

But Buddha began to set off towards the road out of the village. 'You must not go that way,' the people called. 'Sometimes we have sent as many as forty men together for safety and none of them has ever come back.'

But the Buddha continued on his way.

And as he left the poor village and passed by the weedy fields he understood why the villagers all looked afraid and why their houses were broken.

After travelling along the country road for some time Buddha heard a sound of laughing behind him. Turning round he saw the Robber Finger-Necklace. It was enough to look at him to make you afraid. He was a large man marked with many scars of battle. He carried so large a bow that most men would not have been able to bend it let alone shoot one of the many arrows he carried on his back. Hanging from his great leather belt was an enormous heavy sword. Robber Finger-Necklace was laughing because he was looking forward to a bit of cruel fun with this monk who was silly enough to walk alone along this road. And as the robber laughed he shook the strange necklace around his neck. It was the necklace strung with the fingers of his murdered victims.

Buddha quietly turned and carried on his way. With a mouthful of foul language Finger-Necklace began to chase after him. He made a great dash forward and drew his sword to lunge at the Buddha. But he was not quite near enough. Buddha kept walking slowly along the road. Finger-Necklace charged again with all his strength, but wouldn't quite catch up. It seemed that however fast he ran he wouldn't beat the Buddha's slow walking.

'Stand still, monk!' shouted the angry robber. 'Stand still, will you! I have chased after horses and even elephants and caught up with them. I have raced against deer and the fastest chariots and nothing ever escapes from me. Stand still!'

'Oh but I *am* standing still,' said Buddha, 'and if you want to catch me up, you must learn to stand still too.'

Robber Finger-Necklace was completely puzzled by these strange words and indeed he did stand still as the Buddha began to explain. 'By rushing about you will never really get anywhere,' he said, 'but if you stand still, if you let your mind stand still and be calm, you will find that you will really begin to get somewhere. So I am standing still and I am getting somewhere; you are rushing round like mad and you are not getting anywhere at all.'

Finger-Necklace looked into the peaceful calm eyes of the Buddha and understood. He threw his sword and his bow and his arrows as far away as he could and quietly walked behind the Buddha.

When they came back to Savatthi Buddha shaved the head of his new monk Angulimala and gave him a yellow robe to wear. And they went out into the city to preach.

As they passed through the streets a great army of 5000 soldiers on horseback passed by. In their midst was the King's own carriage. When King Pasenadi saw the famous teacher, he called to the soldiers to stop. The King stepped from his carriage and explained to the Buddha what was going on.

'I ask for your blessing, holy one,' said King Pasenadi. 'The people of this city have come to me to beg me to save them from the cruel Robber Finger-Necklace. He is a man with no kindness in him whatever who kills and robs them and burns their houses. And no-one has ever managed to get the better of him. Give me your blessing that I may succeed.'

'What would you say,' said Buddha, 'if I brought the Robber Finger-Necklace here before you with his head shaved as a monk and wearing the yellow robes?'

'If you could manage to do that,' replied the King, 'I should be happy to shake his hand and put food into his begging bowl. But even you couldn't change a man as cruel as Finger-Necklace.'

'This monk Angulimala was the Robber Finger-Necklace,' said Buddha.

The poor King trembled when he heard this and looked at the scars on the face and body of the monk who stood beside the Buddha. But when he looked into his eyes and saw a calmness in them more peaceful than he knew himself, he felt more at ease.

'This monk Angulimala has made the Buddhist vow to hurt no living thing and to show kindness to all things,' said Buddha.

The King called his army to halt and spent some time with Buddha and Finger-Necklace talking. 'With my 5000 soldiers I was afraid because I was sure I would not be able to beat Robber Finger-Necklace,' said King Pasenadi, 'and yet you have been able to capture him with something far stronger than the sword.'

'It is impossible for anyone to control the mind of anyone else,' replied the Buddha, 'but anyone can learn to control their own self.'

*

The Buddha said:

The person who didn't care at all,
if he cares *now*, he lights up the world
as when the moon escapes from behind a cloud.

Whatever wicked things you have done in the past,
if you do good *now*, you light up the world
as when the moon escapes from behind a cloud.

(*from the* Dhammapada 172-173)

*

Ditch diggers lead the water where it should go,
arrow makers cut their arrows straight and true,
carpenters plane the wood flat and smooth;
wise men learn to control themselves.

(*from the* Dhammapada 80)

*

The Buddha and Elder Dhammarama

The Buddha had been born as a rich prince in a luxurious Indian palace, but he found that luxury still left something wanting in his heart. He lived as a holy man starving his body of food for many many months and found that this did not give him the answer. At last he found understanding. He realised that it was no use worrying about the things of this world, because all of them changed and eventually died. By understanding this and by searching for a peace within yourself, we can come to understand as Buddha had understood and set our souls free.

When Buddha understood he could happily have left this earth for ever, but he felt such kindness towards other people that he travelled around for many years trying to make other people see the truth as he had seen it.

But when Buddha was nearly eighty years old he announced to his followers that the time was coming when he must die. As the news spread many hundreds of monks and other people came to visit him for the last time on the foothills of the Himalayas in the town of Kusinagara. They paid their last respects to the man who had taught them so much.

'You must not cry for me. All living things must die. Besides you will still have the words I have taught you and these will never die. Just follow my teachings; they are your master now.'

There were many who were very upset because the Buddha was dying. Some of the monks knelt every day at his side. Amongst them were some who noticed that Elder Dhammarama was missing. Dhammarama had been one of Buddha's loyal followers for many years past and had hardly ever left his side. And yet as the great man was about to die Dhammarama was nowhere to be seen.

Some of the monks complained to Buddha that Dhammarama was not being as loyal to him as they were. But Buddha understood.

In fact, Dhammarama had gone away to spend time on his own. He had followed the Buddha for many years and listened to his teaching. But now the Buddha was near to death Dhammarama realised that he had not managed to do as the Buddha said. Buddha had always taught that all livings things must die and that everything in this life changes. And yet here was Dhammarama hoping never to lose his friend, the Buddha. Dhammarama realised that he had not really understood the Buddha's teaching in his heart if he felt like that. And so in a quiet place he was trying to understand and follow the Buddha's teaching rather than worry about the Buddha dying.

Buddha knew this. He said to the monks who complained: 'There are people who bring me flowers and sweet-smelling perfumes and other gifts, but they do not really honour me. And there are people who try to follow what I have taught them, they are the people who really honour me.'

*

Buddhists believe that we can all become buddhas if we follow the teachings of the Buddha and live each new life better than the last. Elder Dhammarama understood this better than the other monks. The following was written by the missionary Padma-Sambhava who took Buddhist teachings from India to Tibet in 747 CE.

Oil is made from sesame seeds and butter is made from milk; but you don't get oil or butter until the sesame seeds have been pressed and the milk has been churned. In the same way all living beings are buddhas, but they will never find peace until they realise this.

(*from the writings of Padma-Sambhava*)

*

The Chinese

Monkey

Monkey, Sun Hou Tzu, appears in the legends associated with the pilgrimage of the Buddhist monk, Hsuan Tsung from China to India in the 7th century CE to bring back the scriptures of Mahayana Buddhism. Hsuan Tsung, a historical personage, is usually known as Tripitaka (the Three Baskets of Scripture) after the holy books with which he returned. After a number of outrageous exploits on earth and in heaven, Monkey was condemned by the Buddha to assist Tripitaka in his arduous journey overland to India in order to gain forgiveness and ultimately salvation.

*

Monkey on the Buddha's hand

In the east of China on the Mountain of Flowers and Fruit stood a rock that had been there since the world began. The pure rain of heaven and the fresh breezes of the earth, the light of the sun and moon made the rock split open — and out burst Monkey.

Monkey ran and leapt about the world discovering all he could. He used his sharp eyes and ears, his clever hands and his keen brain. He led the monkey tribe to the Mountain of Flowers and Fruit and there they lived a life of luxury with plenty to eat and enjoy. Monkey was their king.

The years passed and each day was the same. The monkeys played and ate and drank and slept and they were all happy.

But Monkey grew bored. He began to realise that he would spend all his days in the same way and then he would die. He would have done nothing with his life. So Monkey decided that he must discover the secret of living forever.

Across the sea he sailed until he came to the Southern Land where the humans live. But the people there spent all their time making money and he could learn nothing from them. Monkey sailed on until he reached the Western Land and here he met an old priest who knew the ways of the world and of heaven. Monkey became his pupil.

For many years Monkey studied with the wise old priest. He could change himself into seventy two different shapes; he could make himself invisible; he could ride on clouds; metal could not stop him nor stone; water could not drown him nor fire burn him; Monkey now understood the laws of nature and would live forever.

It was not long, however, before Monkey began to get up to his monkey tricks. He enjoyed showing off to the other students by turning himself into different things. One day the old priest caught all the other students laughing and joking instead of working. But he could not find Monkey anywhere. The joke was that Monkey had turned himself into a tree next to where the priest stood. The priest had had enough. He sent Monkey back home, telling him to cause no more trouble.

But Monkey did not stay peacefully at home for long. On one adventure he visited the Dragon King in his palace beneath the sea. He stole a magic iron rod which he used as a weapon. On another adventure he visited the Land of the Dead and crossed out his name and the names of all the monkey tribe from the Book of the Dead so that they would all live forever.

The Dragon King and the King of the Dead both sent official complaints to the Emperor of Jade, King of Heaven. They demanded that something be done about this monkey who did not know how to behave himself.

The Jade Emperor decided that they should be kind to Monkey, unless he got up to mischief again. He was invited to live in heaven with the gods.

And so Monkey went to live in heaven. For a time all was peaceful. Monkey ate and drank as much as he wanted and enjoyed himself very much. But he soon became bored again.

So Monkey took a stroll around the Peach Garden where grew the peaches of the Queen of Heaven. Whoever ate these peaches would be sure never to die. And then he sneaked into the banqueting hall where the Queen of Heaven was going to hold a great feast. Monkey ate all the food and drank all the wine and left the place in a terrible mess.

It took the whole army of heaven to capture Monkey and bring him before the Jade Emperor. The Jade Emperor did not know what to do with such a badly-behaved creature and sent for the Buddha to come and deal with him.

'So you're the King of the monkeys, are you?' said the Buddha angrily.

'King of the monkeys, and King of Heaven!' shouted Monkey fiercely.

'The Emperor of Jade has been leading a perfect life for the past hundred million years. What makes you think that *you* are fit to take his throne?'

'I can turn myself into seventy two different shapes,' answered Monkey, 'and I can do a somersault through the clouds a hundred thousand miles in one go.'

'I'll have a bet with you then, Monkey,' laughed the Buddha. 'If you are so clever, jump off my right hand. If you do it, you shall have the throne of Heaven. If you cannot, you must go back to earth and show you are sorry for your sins.'

'It's a deal,' laughed Monkey. 'Let's start now.'

The Buddha held out his right hand and Monkey stepped onto it. With a tremendous leap Monkey hurled himself into the air so fast that no-one could see him move. He was flying through the air at a tremendous speed. Through the clouds, past the planets and stars and into the regions of space where there was nothing at all flew Monkey, until at last he came to five huge pillars which rose up so high that Monkey could not see the tops of them.

'These great pillars must mark the end of the world,' said Monkey. 'And Buddha thought I wouldn't be able to jump off his hand!' To prove that he'd been there, Monkey scratched his name on the middle pillar. 'Monkey was here,' he wrote. Then with another mighty somersault he flew back to where he had come from.

'I flew to the very end of the world,' said Monkey as he landed beside the Buddha. 'And to prove it I wrote my name on one of the five great pillars that stand there.'

'You have been in the palm of my hand all the time,' Buddha answered seriously. 'Look!'

Monkey looked, and there on the middle finger he read the words, 'Monkey was here.'

'The universe is bigger than you know, Monkey,' said the Buddha. 'There are many things that you do not know and many powers that you do not understand. And now for your punishment.'

Buddha held Monkey firmly in his hand and closed his fingers around him. And as he did so, his hand became a mountain with five peaks. Buddha reached out of the western gate of Heaven and placed the mountain, with Monkey inside it, down on to the earth. And here the proud Monkey king had to stay until the time of his punishment was over and he was able at last to show how sorry he was for his sins.

*

Many of the great Chinese thinkers believed that people spend too much time learning about religion or filling their minds with knowledge. They thought that we should simply open our minds and let the Truth fill them. After his punishment Monkey helps a Buddhist priest bring back the holy books from India to China. When the Buddha gives them the scrolls, however, they have nothing on them.

The Buddha said: 'As a matter of fact, it is blank scrolls like these that are the true holy writings. But I realise that the people of China are too foolish and ignorant to believe it, so there is nothing to do but to give them some scrolls with writing on.'

(from Monkey, Sun Hou Tzu *by Wu Cheng En)*

*

Stop talking, stop thinking,
  and you will understand everything.
There is no need to look for the Truth;
  just empty your mind of ideas.

(from the writings of Seng Tsan in the Taisho Issaikyo, the Chinese Tripitake)

*

Lei Kung, My Lord Thunder

The Taoist Heaven reflects the earthly governmental organisation of Imperial China with ministries and ministers and a whole range of beaurocrats in a strict hierarchy, responsible ultimately to the August Supreme Emperor of Jade, Yu Huang Shang Ti, also known as Father of Heaven, Lao Tien Yeh. But the priestly conception of the divine order and that of the people do not always coincide, as in the case of the Ministry of Thunder. Classically there are a number of divinities responsible for various functions within the ministry, but popular recognition is given only to one god of thunder, Lei Kung. Not only is he in charge of making thunder noises during storms, but he carries out punishments on behalf of Father of Heaven on undetected criminals, earthly or otherwise. There are no temples to Lei Kung and no one prays to him unless it is to wreak righteous vengeance on an enemy.

*

Lei Kung, My Lord Thunder

Making storms is a complicated business for the Chinese gods. Orders are issued by the Dragon King as to where the storm must happen and how much thunder and lightning and rain there must be. First the Little Cloud Boy, Yun T'ung heaps up the rain clouds ready for Mrs Wind, Feng Po Po who gallops around on a tiger stirring them all up. Yu Tzu, the Master of Rain, sprinkles the rain from his great sword which he dips into an enormous pot full of water. Flashes of lightning are made by Mother Lightning, Tien Mu using mirrors, while the rumble of thunder comes from My Lord Thunder, Lei Kung.

Lei Kung, the thunder god is horribly ugly. His skin is blue, he has wings, and for hands and feet he has fierce claws. Around his waist hang large drums which he hammers to make the noise of the thunder. In his hands he carries a hammer and chisel. These are to punish the wicked.

Lord Thunder acts as a heavenly policeman for the Father of Heaven, Lao Tien Yeh. If there are human beings who have committed crimes that have not been spotted, or if there are spirits who like to harm the people of earth, the Father of Heaven sends Lei Kung to punish them with his hammer and chisel.

One day a hunter was out in the forest when a terrific storm blew up. He sheltered under a large tree and waited for the storm to pass. But the lightning kept flashing at the tree and the thunder rolled around the same place and didn't move on.

The hunter looked up into the tree and was most astonished to see a young child clinging to the topmost branches. The child was holding a stick with a dirty old rag tied to it like a flag and he kept waving it at the thunder and lightning. Now it is very well known in China that My Lord Thunder does not like unclean things, so every time he tried to pass the child he was forced to move back from the dirty rag.

It is also very well known in China that the Thunder God only punishes people who deserve to be punished, so the hunter decided that he had to help him. Fitting an arrow to his bow he took aim. He could not bring himself to shoot at the child, so he aimed at the flag instead. The arrow flew straight towards the flag and knocked it out of the child's hand.

There was a mighty flash of lightning, and a great crack of thunder. The tree was hit and the hunter sent flying. When he came to his senses again the storm had passed. Lying at the foot of the tree was the dead body of a huge and terrible lizard. This, and not the young child, was the real shape of an evil spirit that had now been punished by Heaven.

In his hand the hunter found a small roll of paper. Opening it up he read, 'Many thanks from Lei Kung, Lord of Thunder. You will now live twelve years longer for helping with the work of Heaven.'

*

The Chinese believe that the Tao (the Way of Heaven) is there for all to follow. Of course, not everyone does follow it.

My words are very easy to know,
    and very easy to follow.
But not all the people in the world know them,
    nor do they follow them.
It is because some people know *too much*

that they do not know me.

(from the Tao Te Ching *seventy, attributed to Lao Tzu)*

*

The True Way has always been here in the world and has never died. It is here in the minds of people: some of them take no notice of it, while others follow it carefully. That is why the Way is sometimes brilliantly clear, and at other times it is hard to see.

(from the Chou Li *attributed to Chou Kung, Duke of Chou)*

*

The Dragon Gods

Yu Huang Shang Ti, the August Supreme Emperor of Jade sends down his orders from Heaven for the distribution of rain to the four Lung Wang, the Dragon Kings of North, South, East and West who live in wonderful submarine palaces. They pass their orders through their ministers and officials to the lesser dragon gods whose homes are to be found in rivers and lakes, in streams, ponds and wells near to which the local populace have usually placed a shrine or small temple. To a rural population rainfall is clearly of the utmost importance. The dragon gods would be praised and entreated in times of drought. Sometimes their statues even were maltreated to encourage them to plead on the peasants' behalf with the Jade Emperor. The dragons generally followed orders from Heaven to the letter (they were subject to severe punishment if they didn't), however they could exercise a certain measure of discretion, and favour those who deserved advancement.

*

Wu and the Yellow Dragon God

Wu was the son of Yin, a poor Chinese farmer. As Wu sat outside their small cottage one day, there came along the road a young noble man dressed all in yellow and riding a magnificent horse. Four servants walked with him, two in front and two behind, one of them carrying an umbrella to shade their lord from the sun.

Wu was very surprised indeed. It was a rare thing to see anybody on the road in so poor a district. His mouth fell open and his eyes grew wide at the brilliance of the scene.

The noble pulled up his horse in front of Wu's house and said, 'Hello, Wu, son of Yin. Could I stay at your cottage to rest a while before I go on my way?'

'Certainly, my Lord,' answered Wu, wondering how the young man knew his name. Wu called his father and grandmother and took the lord and his four servants inside. They treated their guests politely and although they didn't have much to eat, they shared what they had. After the young noble man and his servants had eaten and rested and the horse had been watered and fed, the young lord thanked Wu and his family for their kindness. Wu noticed that the servant with the umbrella carried it upside-down as he went out through the gate.

'I'll see you again tomorrow,' called the lord as he set off along the road. Wu stood and watched. The lord rode slowly off towards the west, towards a great bank of rainclouds. And as he journeyed up the distant hills, he seemed to rise up and disappear into the clouds.

When Wu came back into the cottage his father asked him if he had noticed anything strange about their guests. 'I did,' said Wu. 'None of them had any seams in his clothes, and the horse had five spots of different colours on him, and instead of hair he had scales. When they walked their feet did not quite touch the ground.'

'They are spirits of some kind,' said the wise old grandmother. 'I think the young lord may well have been a dragon god. We could be in for rain tonight.' Grandma went to bed, while Wu and his father, Yin stayed up to pray for their safety. And outside the storm clouds were gathering.

No-one saw the sun come up at dawn the next day. Heavy clouds filled the sky, and as the small family ate their small breakfast, the rain started to pour down. Streams and rivers were filled to overflowing and the waters poured over the fields and houses.

As the flood swept across the whole valley, people and cattle gathered for safety on the hills. It rained throughout the whole day, and by night-time the tiny cottage was entirely surrounded by floodwater.

Yin was worried that the farm would be next to disappear under the water but the boy, Wu told him they would be safe. 'Do you remember I saw one of the lord's servants carrying the umbrella upside-down through our gate? I think that was a sign that we would be protected from the storm.'

Wu signed to his father to be quiet. Thunder rolled and the pouring rain could be heard all around − except on their own roof. Wu leaned out of the window and looked up at the clouds. Although it was nearly as dark as night, he could just make out the shape of a great yellow dragon hovering over their small house. And no rain fell in the shadow of the dragon.

At midday the rain stopped and the clouds slowly began to roll away. And as the flood waters went down it could be seen that great damage had been done to all the countryside, but Yin's tiny cottage and small farm were perfectly alright. The storm had not touched them.

Later that afternoon Wu saw the noble youth dressed in yellow come riding back on his magnificent horse, two servants behind and two in front. 'I said I would come back today,' said the young lord. 'I have come to thank you for giving me food and rest yesterday.' He leaned forward and plucked a golden scale from the horse's neck and handed it to Wu. And then slowly he made his way along the road to the east from where he had come the day before.

Wu looked at the golden scale which shone like sunlight.

Some time later Wu and his family had a message from the Emperor of China. He had heard how the farm had been protected by a dragon god and wanted to meet the boy. Wu took his golden scale with him in a small box. When the Emperor asked to see the scale, Wu opened the box and the scale lit up the whole room and brought a feeling of happiness and peace to all who were there. Wu found that his scale gave him the power to make wise decisions and to cure many diseases. The Emperor made Wu one of his government and before the boy had grown into a man he had made himself rich and happy and one of the Emperor's wisest ministers.

*

The Chinese believe that gods and men all must follow the Tao (the Way of Heaven) if they are to find everlasting peace.

The Way of Heaven has no body or shape,
   but it made and cares for heaven and earth.
The Way of Heaven has no feelings,
   but it makes the sun and moon move as they do.
The Way of Heaven has no name,
   but it makes things grow and run smoothly.
I do not know its name, but if I try hard,
   I will call it the Tao, the Way of Heaven.

The true and everlasting Way of Heaven.
People who understand will naturally find it.
And people who find it will live in perfect peace.

(from the Classic of Purity, the Khing Kang King 1: 1 and 2: 3 by Ko Yuan)

*

Wang Shuh and the Black Dragon God

Wang Shuh was a herbalist. He knew all about the plants that grew near his village and which ones he could use to cure illness. He was good at his job, but he never made very much money, for the people of the village were poor and didn't have much to give.

One hot summer day Wang Shuh set off up the mountain to find the red cloud herb, a rather rare plant that could cure all sorts of diseases. He climbed higher and higher until the sun was shining overhead and then he stopped for something to eat. He sat down in the shade of some trees by a clear deep pool. A waterfall splashed into the pool, the birds sang and Wang Shuh felt very peaceful as he ate his small meal of rice.

As he gazed into the waters of the pool he could see something moving down below. He leaned forward to get a better look and could make out the shape of a big red carp slowly weaving about. On its back was a tiny blue boy no bigger than a child's forearm. In his hand he carried a blue rush which he waved as the fish swam up and down and around under the water.

The fish and the boy moved back and forth slowly coming nearer to the surface of the water, until at last with a gentle splash came right of the water and up into the air. Wang Shuh watched as they rose higher, up above the top of the mountain and into a thick bank of dark cloud that was beginning to cover the sky.

Once Wang Shuh had got over the shock, he remembered he had a job to do and set off once more for the top of the mountain where he hoped he would find the rare red cloud herb. But at the top of the mountain there was nothing to be found. Wang Shuh looked all around him. Way below he could see the small village where he lived. Far in the distance he could see the Eastern Sea. The clouds hung heavy in that direction and they were moving nearer. Wang Shuh realised there was going to be a storm and started to make his way down again. Suddenly there was a great crack and a flash of bright lightning lit up the dark thunderclouds. And then the rain started.

Wang Shuh dashed to shelter inside an old hollow tree as the storm broke. And in the middle of the pouring rain, the flashes of lightning and the rolls of thunder Wang Shuh could make out something weaving about in the clouds. It was an enormous black thunder dragon moving up and down and around in the heart of the storm. And as it moved back and forth spitting out fiery lightning and roaring out thunder, Wang Shuh saw that it held in its claw a blue rush. The dragon was the small blue boy and the red carp.

As the rain water overflowed from the streams and began to fill the valley, Wang Shuh began to get frightened and started to make his way down the mountain. As he came to the trees by the waterfall, the rain stopped. He could hear sweet music. He stopped and peered through the branches to the pool. Down through the air came the red carp with the tiny blue boy on its back. Down and down until with a gentle splash boy and fish went into the water. Deeper and deeper they sank until they were out of sight.

Wang Shuh was just going to leave the place when he noticed that the edges of the pool were smothered by a plant which had not been there before. Taking a closer look he saw that it was the precious red cloud herb he had come in search of. It was growing everywhere.

Wang Shuh stuffed as much as he could into his bag, into his pockets, up his sleeves and inside his jacket, and happily skipped down the mountain to his village. Wang Shuh was able to cure the people of the village of practically anything with his wonderful herb and soon he became famous roundabout as the herbalist who could cure all illness. When the Emperor came to hear of Wang Shuh, he sent for him to cure his daughter who was suffering from a mysterious disease that none of his doctors had been able to cure. Wang Shuh's red cloud herb did the trick and the Emperor made him the Royal Doctor. Wang Shuh became rich and famous and he lived to a ripe old age.

*

Heaven wants people to love and help each other;
  it does not want them to hate and bully.
How do we know this?
  Because Heaven loves all people and gives them
  all good things.
How do we know that Heaven cares for everyone?
  Because Heaven has given us food.
In the world there are no countries big or small:
  they all belong to Heaven.
As for people, there are no old or young people,
  no masters and no slaves;
  they are all children of Heaven. . .
So, if Heaven cares for everyone
  and gives enough food for everyone,
  Heaven must want people to love and help each other.

(from the Mo Tzu Book of Mo Ti)

*

The Gods of the Earth

In pre-revolutionary mainland China the Emperor in Peking made spring and autumn sacrifices on behalf of his people to propitiate the gods of the Earth. But the rural peasantry also worshipped gods outside the official pantheon. There were gods covering most aspects of their agricultural lives: gods of weather, cereals, and cattle; there was a pig god, an ox god, a goddess protector of silkworms, *and so on. There were (and still are in Hong Kong and Taiwan) many local soil deities whose recognition exists within a very limited area. The hierarchy in Heaven was a replica of that on earth, and the behaviour and character of the gods was very human.*

*

The wise god and the foolish god

The Chinese think of their gods as being very much like humans. They are sometimes loving and kind like parents, sometimes they are old and wise like grand-parents. Sometimes they are powerful and angry like kings, and sometimes poor and weak like peasants. And there are clever gods and foolish gods.

In a lonely part of China stand two mountains, the South Mountain and the North Mountain. On each mountain is a small shrine built for a god of the earth. Many years ago the farmers who had lived in those parts had built the shrines and placed statues of the gods there. The gods were given offerings of food, they were kept painted and polished, cleaned and dressed. Incense was burned before before them and hymns were sung to them. In return the gods made sure that the crops grew well and that the farmers' animals were fat and healthy. But no-one now lived nearby and the two gods were left alone and never given anything.

'I'm always hungry nowadays,' said the North god to the South god one day.

'So am I,' said the South god. 'We must do something about it.' The South god sat down and thought and at last came up with a plan.

One day the son of a wealthy farmer happened to pass by the shrine of the South god. As he passed, the god touched him. The god had put a curse on the boy so that as soon as he got home, he grew ill with a fever. His temperature was high and he sweated and shivered at the same time. As the family stood around the boy's bed watching him get worse by the minute, there came the voice of the South god, booming down from the mountain, saying, 'Boil up a piece of camphor wood from near my shrine. Let the boy drink this medicine and he shall be cured.'

Immediately the rich farmer set off for the South Mountain. He bowed respect-fully before the statue of the god. Growing close to the shrine there was indeed a camphor tree. The farmer broke off a small branch and hurried home. He boiled up the wood as he had been told and gave his son a drink of the hot liquid. Almost as soon as he had swallowed it, the boy sat up, and within half an hour he was perfectly well again.

The family were so happy that they dressed in their best clothes and went together to the South mountain shrine to offer thanks to the god. They tidied up the shrine and dressed the god's statue. They lit candles and burned sweet-smelling incense, and they left offerings of the many types of food that they grew on the farm. As they went back down the mountain, the god of the South was well-fed and well-pleased.

The god on the North Mountain had been watching all this time and shouted across to his brother god, 'That was a good idea. I'll do the same.'

Some time later a peasant boy came past the shrine of the North Mountain. As he passed, the god touched him. As soon as the boy got back to his poor peasant hut, he was taken ill with a fever. The North god shouted down from his mountain, 'Boil up a piece of camphor wood from near my shrine. Let the boy drink this medicine and he shall be cured.'

The poor boy's father set off for the North Mountain. But when he came to the shrine of the god, he could see no camphor tree. The only camphor wood he could see was the wood the statue was made of. He guessed the god must have meant him to cut off a piece of his own statue. Not wanting to damage the god's statue, he lifted up its long robe and cut a piece off the top of one of its legs.

He went back home and gave his son the medicine made from the camphor wood and the boy got better.

Up on the North mountain the god waited for his food and presents. But the peasant family did not come. Certainly they were pleased that their son had been cured, but they were so poor that they had nothing to give the god.

Angry and limping, the god of the North hobbled over to swear and curse at his brother. But the god of the South Mountain did not have any sympathy: 'It's your own fault,' he laughed. 'You should have made sure the boy was from a rich family. And you really should have checked to see if there was a camphor tree near your shrine. If you get hurt because of your own stupidity, it's no use blaming other people.'

*

There were many shrines and temples in China. Some were great and magnificent like the Temple of Heaven in Peking where the Emperor performed sacrifices in spring, summer, winter and autumn on behalf of the people of China. It is said to have the largest altar in the world (70 m in diameter) and can still be seen. There were temples in towns and villages, small shrines in people's houses, and there were those that were used every day and those that were forgotten.

Here is the hymn that was sung at the Temple of Heaven, after the offering of the wine, while the Emperor placed the cooked meats on the altar. The hymn is sung to Shang Ti, the greatest god.

I bring solemn offerings
    to be blessed by Heaven.
The flames of the sacrifice rise up
    as a prayer to Heaven.
Only the Holy One can receive the sacrifice.
The God of Heaven sits in a chariot

pulled by six dragons.
They fly up through purple mists.
May I follow the rule of Heaven
  throughout my large empire.

(Sacrificial Hymn sung at the Winter Sacrifice from the Shih Ching, the
Book of Songs*)*

*

Wen Chang, the God of Books

*Imperial China was intensely bureaucratic and success depended on the passing
of examinations. Wen Chang as god of literature had overall charge of the heavenly
ministry, but greater popular acclaim was offered to his assistant, Kuei Hsing,
god of examinations, represented as an ugly man holding a writing brush and a
measuring tub. The brush is to mark on the list of candidates the names of the
successful to be presented to the August Supreme Emperor of Jade. The measure
is to weigh the talents of all. In China the star sign of the Plough was called 'the
Northern Bushel', these being Kuei Hsing's stars. Literate Chinese families would
have images or shrines dedicated to one or other of these gods in their houses.*

*

Wen Chang and the student

China of old was run by a great army of people working in offices. They all had
to be able to read and write properly and so they were tested every year by the
Emperor's inspectors. If anyone wanted to get a job in an office, they too had
to sit for examinations. Not only were they tested on earth, but also in Heaven.

Wen Chang, the god of books and his assistant, Kuei Hsing, the god of examinations, made sure that all the hard-working students passed their exams, and that
all the lazy ones failed. There was a god called Red Jacket who could sometimes
help students who hadn't worked as hard as they should have done. When Kuei

Hsing is checking through the list of names to be given to the Emperor of Heaven, Red Jacket can sometimes get an extra name added to the list by saying nice things about the student. But it is certainly safer to work hard and make sure that you pass that way!

There lived in Ancient China a young student. He had worked hard all through school and college. His parents were very proud of him. The student had applied for a job in one of the Emperor's government offices and the time had come for his examination.

The student sat down at his desk with all the others taking the exam. He had his paper, his writing brush and his ink ready. And then the examiner read out the questions for them to answer and the exam began.

Some students started writing straight away knowing exactly what to do. Others weren't quite so sure and had to keep stopping to think. There were one or two who had written only their name on the paper and nothing else. Our hard-working student wrote solidly for three hours until the examiner told them to stop.

How differently the students went home afterwards. Some chatted and laughed, others skipped and danced. Some trudged home miserably, while others pretended that they didn't care. Our student walked home more and more slowly. As he walked he began to realise that he hadn't quite understood some of the questions. He had written some rather silly answers. By the time he reached his house he was disappointed and cross with himself. He had worked and studied hard for many years for this examination, and now he had ruined his chances.

Before he went to bed that night he prayed to Wen Chang, the god of books, for help. At last he managed to get to sleep. And while he slept he dreamed. He dreamed that Wen Chang came to him. The god sat reading the answer papers from the exam. Some papers he put to one side, others he threw into the fire. The student saw Wen Chang read his paper, and throw it into the fire with the others.

But when the god had read all the papers he reached into the fire and took out the crumbled and burnt ashes of the student's papers. And has he unfolded them they became whole again!

Wen Chang handed the papers back to the student, and when he read them he saw that many of his answers had been changed. These were the answers he should have written. The student read the answers again and again until he knew them off by heart. The vision of the god disappeared.

When our student woke up the next morning a messenger brought news that the examination hall had been burned down during the night, and all the students' answer papers with it. All students were asked to come to sit the examination again.

This time the student remembered the answers that the god, Wen Chang had given him. And he passed. However, if the student had not been such a hard worker, the ending to the story might have been quite different.

*

It isn't always easy to know what you should or shouldn't do. This prayer was written for a young king of China nearly 3000 years ago.

Praise him. Praise him.
The Way of Heaven is clear
But it is hard to do what God wants.
He is not high up and far away;
He goes up and he comes down
And every day he sees what we do.
I am still young
And not very clever,
But day by day
I search for the light of wisdom.
Help me to carry my troubles
And show me the Way of Life.

(from the Chou Li*)*

*

The Hindus

Indra

Indra was worshipped by the nomadic Aryan invaders of India from very early times. During the period of their immigration in the 3rd century BCE Indra typified the warrior caste. He was a demon-fighting, heavy-drinking, quick-tempered noble; he is king of the lesser gods; he is the fertility god who brings rain and life to the dry land; he is the embodiment of what the Aryans saw as a good leader. To Indra are dedicated a quarter of the thousand priestly hymns of the Rig Veda whose oral tradition dates back many centuries before its first written form in about 1000 BCE . In later times Indra and the other thirty-three lesser gods have very much taken second place to the great triad of Brahma, Vishnu and Shiva who themselves are seen in philosophical Hinduism as aspects of the Supreme Principle of the universe, Brahman, whose nature is so undefinable that ordinary people need to approach it through the medium of one of the gods. In the story of Indra's conflict with the demon Viritra the god shows a human face which is typical and which formerly endeared him to his devotees.

Indra kills the demon Viritra

Indra is the king of the gods of the Indian Heaven. He rides through the clouds on a great elephant and, as he passes, the flash of lightning and the crash of the thunder bring rain which gives life to the dry land. Indra is a warrior god always ready to fight against evil to protect gods and men.

There rose up in the ancient past a great serpent called Viritra. Viritra breathed fire and scorched the earth to a dry and dusty desert where nothing could live. And as the sun rises in the morning and grows in strength throughout the day, so did Viritra grow. He towered high over the earth and burned the heavens with his hot breath. And his heart was full of hatred for Indra.

Indra came to kill the dragon who seemed to be swallowing the whole universe. And as Indra stood before him ready for battle Viritra opened wide his enormous mouth into an evil smile. And swallowed Indra.

The gods were shocked. The serpent had swallowed their mightiest warrior. Who would it swallow next? Quickly they talked about what they could do. If Indra had not been able to fight the creature none of them would stand a chance. A bit of trickery was needed.

The thirty-three gods created a spell to make the monster yawn. While it yawned perhaps the king of the gods could scramble out. The spell was cast. For a long time nothing happened. And then Viritra began to close his eyes and open his mouth. Wider and wider he yawned until it seemed as if he would swallow the whole universe. But no-one can swallow when they are yawning. Out from the dragon's fiery mouth like a flash of lightning shot the warrior god, Indra. He was free again.

As soon as he had finished yawning the serpent gave a mighty roar of anger. The battle continued over the earth and into space. Indra swept across vast distances and the great dragon lumbered clumsily after him. Clouds of fire and smoke were hurled across the face of the stars and the noise of the desperate struggle could be heard by the gods in Heaven. And the harder the fight the more Viritra's strength and size grew. Indra realised that he could not win against such an enemy and decided that he must leave the battle before he was swallowed again. He would have to think of something else.

Indra and the other gods decided that they must visit the great god Vishnu. Vishnu is the Ruler of the Universe, the Lord of the Worlds. Vishnu it was who made Indra the king of the gods of Heaven; Vishnu is worshipped by the gods. And Vishnu is everywhere in the universe; he is inside every thing.

'O Great God,' said Indra, standing very small before Vishnu's mighty power, 'the whole universe is in danger of being swallowed up by a dragon of great evil. We gods of Heaven are not able to defeat this monster and we have come to beg for your help.'

'I shall give you my advice and my help,' replied Vishnu. 'I shall do what is best for you and for men. You must first go and talk with the priests and the wise men. They will make a truce between you and the serpent Viritra. And when the time is ready, Indra, I shall help you kill the beast.'

The gods left the mighty Vishnu and went straight away to see the priests and the wise men. Quickly a truce was arranged with Viritira so that they could talk. And after a great deal of discussion and argument it was agreed that Viritra would live in peace and harm no-one. Indra had to agree that he would not harm the dragon with anything dry or anything liquid, nor with stone nor wood, neither with a weapon nor with his thunderbolt, not by day nor by night.

But Indra was not happy. He felt as though he had been made to give in to evil. And although there was peace on earth the air was hot and heavy. Great dark clouds hung overhead but no rain fell to cool the burning earth and bring life to plants and animals.

One evening, just after the sun had set below the western horizon, Indra saw the dragon dragging its huge body along the seashore. The clouds glowed red from the setting sun and the air was hot with Viritra's fiery breath. Indra suddenly realised that it was neither day nor night. The sun had set but it was not yet dark. Out at sea a whirlwind had blown up a tall column of foam. It was not a weapon of wood or stone and it was neither dry nor liquid.

Using all his divine power Indra acted quickly. He took hold of the huge swirling mass of foam and hurled it at the monster on the beach. As he did so he felt a power enter into the column of foam that was far greater than his own. It was Vishnu. There was a flash of lighning that lit up the whole sky and tremendous crack of thunder as the foam column hit Viritra. A giant scream of agony echoed round the clouds, and smoke belched and steam hissed as Viritra's fires were put out. And as darkness fell the rain began to fall. Cooling rain poured down on the scorched earth to bring life again to the world. The air was fresh and clean and men and gods rested peacefully until morning.

I will tell of the brave things that Indra has done, Indra, the Lord of the Thunder. He killed the dragon and set free the rain, the waters that gushed through mountain valleys in torrents.

Indra, with his own great and deadly thunder, smashed to pieces Viritra, the worst of dragons. Like a tree felled by an axe, Viritra lies dead.

When Indra and the dragon struggled together in battle, the great god won the victory for ever.

Indra is the king of all things that move and all the things that do not move, the king of creatures that are tame and creatures with horns, the Lord of the Thunder. He rules over all living men as their king. Everything is in him as the spokes are within a wheel.

(*from the* Rig Veda *1:32*)

Manu

Manu, whose name means Man, is the progenitor of the human race and the saviour of plants and animals having saved them all from the destruction of a great flood which devastated the whole earth. The story is believed to have an extremely ancient oral tradition dating back to the time before the dispersal of the Indo-European tribes about 5000 years ago. The fish in the story is Matsya, the first incarnation of the great god Vishnu whose role is that of preserver of the universe. Vishnu takes the form of ten different incarnations to maintain order when threatened by the forces of evil. His best known incarnations are those of Rama and Krishna who have a great popular following among Hindus. There have been and will be other Manus for each age of the world. This one, the son of the sun god, was formerly a great king who passed on his kingdom to his son and became a yogi. Granted a boon by God he chose to save the living things of the world from destruction.

Manu and the flood

Manu was the holiest of men. He had been a great and powerful king, but he had given his kingdom and its riches to his son. Manu was a holy man. He owned nothing but the clothes he wore. He ate nothing but what people gave him and he spent his whole life praying to God.

One day as Manu was washing before saying his morning prayers a tiny fish swam into his hands. Manu picked up the fish and put it in a jug. But as the days went by the fish grew. It grew too large for the jug, so Manu put it into a big water-pot. But the fish kept growing until it would not fit in the water-pot. So he took it and put it in a well. And when it had grown too long for the well he took it to a lake. But still the fish kept growing. Manu struggled with the enormous shining fish and hauled it from the lake to the holy River Ganges and from there he took it to the wide ocean. The fish seemed to fill the whole of the sea.

'You are much too powerful to be a demon,' called Manu from the shore. 'You can only be the great god Vishnu who cares for the world, for the creatures and for men.'

'You are right, holy Manu,' came a strong deep voice. 'I am the great god Vishnu, who cares for the universe. As you have cared for men, so shall I care for you.'

The fish told Manu that the world would end in disaster. There would be a terrible drought. No rain would fall and the heat of the sun would dry up all the rivers and lakes. Volcanoes would pour their burning poison on to the earth. Earthquakes would split the land from end to end and all living things would die. Lastly there would come a great flood. The waters of the seas would join together and rise higher and higher until the whole of the earth was covered by sea.

But the fish told Manu that he would be saved because of his goodness. Manu must collect two animals of every kind and seeds of each type of plant and put them into a huge boat which he must build. Then the giant fish sank slowly beneath the waves and was gone.

And what a job Manu was left with! He began the task of building his boat first. It was hard work for Manu. Day after day in the heat of the sun he worked. Day after day with very little water to drink as it had not rained for many months and the land was dry. But at last the boat was finished. Perhaps it looked a little silly standing high above the hot sand, but Manu believed that the flood would soon come, and he started his collection of all the many types of seeds that he could find. And they were all stored carefully on his boat.

Next Manu went out to find two animals of every kind to put into his boat. And they came peacefully and seemed glad to have a place of safety away from the dreadful rumblings and shakings that were beginning to trouble to earth. The sky was covered with hot dark clouds, volcanoes spat red-hot ash high over the land as the world drew to its end.

The sea began to rise. Clouds of steam burst from the hot land as the waters rushed over it. The sea swirled around Manu's boat and quickly it was lifted up and rushed about on waves as high as mountains.

When it seemed certain that the boat would sink Manu's fish poked his enormous head out of the water. He was bigger than ever. He called to Manu to tie a rope around his fin. The fish pulled the boat with its cargo of plants and creatures until Manu could see the top of a mountain sticking up out of the water. It was the peak of one of the Himalaya Mountains.

Here the fish left Manu. 'You must tie the boat to a tree on the mountain as the waters go down. But as the waters get lower you must go down with them,' said the fish. 'You will begin a new race of people on the earth, Manu. They will be known as humans after you.'

The waters slowly drained away and Manu followed them down the side of the mountain until they reached the ground at the bottom. And when the earth could be seen Manu set free the animals and scattered the seeds of many different kinds. And the world began again.

*

Hindus believe that God may take many forms. As Vishnu he has appeared on earth as the Fish, as Rama and as Krishna and in other ways when help was needed. But Hindus believe that the many gods are only parts of one great God. All men and animals, plants and rocks, all the gods, the whole universe are in Him.

He is the One God,
   hidden in all living things and inside everything;
He knows everything that happens,
He watches and knows all we do;
He is the only one.
But he cannot be described.

He made the god Brahma who created the universe;
He taught him the holy books.

I come to God to be saved,
   for God is my place of safety.

(*from the* Svetasvarata Unpanishad *6:11 of the* Yajur-Veda)

*

Krishna

Three great gods reign supreme above the other Hindu gods: they are Brahma the Creator of the universe, Vishnu the Preserver and Shiva the Destroyer. Vishnu has ten incarnations on earth in order to maintain the balance between good and evil which must be kept until Shiva brings an end to this cycle of the universe. The most well-known of these incarnations are those of Rama and Krishna, the seventh and eighth. Worshippers of Krishna practise loving devotion to the god, who is to them the supreme god, all gods, men, and things animate and inanimate. In this story he kills Prince Sisupala who is the third and final incarnation of a demon against whom he fought in previous incarnations, notably when he was Rama and the demon was the ten-headed Ravana. It is said that the demon had formerly been one of Vishnu's high heaven and had been given the choice, after committing an extreme sin, of redeeming himself by living seven incranations as the friend of Vishnu or three incarnations as his enemy. He chose the latter because, despite the suffering involved, he would return to Vishnu all the quicker. This is the aim of Krishna's devotees, to gain release from the cycle of rebirth by completely giving themselves to his service.

Krishna and Sisupala at the coronation sacrifice

There was a time in the world when it looked as if wickedness and evil were going to win. So the great god Vishnu was born as a baby boy called Krishna. His mother was a royal princess, the sister of King Kamsa, a man so evil that many believed him to be a demon. Kamsa was jealous and feared that Krishna would become a danger to him, so he sent his soldiers to kill the new-born child. But when the soldiers arrived they found a baby girl. Secretly that night Krishna's father had swapped his baby boy with a baby girl who belonged to a cowherd outside the city.

Krishna was brought up in a tiny country village looking after the cows. And hardly anyone kew that the poor boy was really a royal prince. Many people realised that the young cowherd was someone rather special, but very few guessed that he was the god Vishnu born on earth.

As Krishna grew into a young man he fought many battles against King Kamsa's wickedness. He met lords and ladies, princes, princesses, kings and queens. He stayed at royal palaces and became famous throughout India.

One day Krishna visited a king and queen whose baby son was called Prince Sisupala. The queen felt that something was not right with her child, though she did not know what it was. She did not know that her baby boy was a demon born into a human family. In the past this demon had committed sins of the utmost wickeness and his heart was full of evil. But the queen did not know this and wanted to protect her son. She asked Krishna, 'My Lord Krishna, give me a wish for the friendship we have.'

'Certainly,' replied Krishna. 'What is your wish?'

'It is a wish for my son,' answered the queen. 'Promise me that you will forgive him if he does anything wrong against you.'

'I will gladly forgive him,' said Krishna. 'Even if he does a hundred things, I will forgive him.'

Sisupala grew into a young man and, as a royal prince, was invited to the great coronation of King Yudhishthira. King Yudhishthira was Krishna's cousin and had made himself the king of all the other kings in India. His coronation was to be a magnificent ceremony. All the kings and queens and princes and princesses, indeed anyone of importance from throughout the land of India, had been invited.

And so the day of the coronation arrived. The many guests were staying in palaces especially built for them. They were large with many rooms and beautifully built. People said they were like the halls of the gods. Priests from every corner of the land had been called and the city was blessed in sacred ceremonies while hymns were sung and prayers were said. Gifts of great value and beauty were given by the guests to King Yudhishthira and he in turn gave presents to the priests and people.

The ceremoney of the coronation was due to begin. Holy fires had been lit and blessed by the priests. King Yudhishthira would stand in the centre of the circle of fires and the high priest would sprinkle him with blessed water and proclaim him King of the Kings of the whole world. And by this sacred and solemn ceremony the land would grow rich in food and the people would do well and be happy.

The ceremony was about to begin and everyone was ready. King Yudhishthira and his family all bowed low to Krishna, when suddenly Sisupala's angry voice could be heard: 'You insult me as a royal prince. And you insult the kings and queens here. How can you, Yudhishthira, King of Kings, bow down before this Krishna. Krishna, the cowherd, brought up among the poor folk in a country village.

Krishna is a nobody and a nothing and yet you honour him in this way.'

The coronation had to stop. Some of the kings were ready to agree with Sisupala. After all, he was right. King Yudhishthira had worshipped Krishna first, and yet they were more royal than he.

Arguments began among the crowd and the calm and seriousness of the great occasion were swept away by loud shouting and the shaking of fists. What could Yudhishthira do to save the day? If the coronation did not go ahead successfully there would be days of darkness and disaster in the land. The King tried to calm Sisupala down, but it was no use. Yudhishthira turned to his old and wise grandfather for his advice. The old man was quietly smiling: 'My Lord Krishna will settle this argument and then the coronation will go on,' he said. 'It seems serious now, but it will not be so later. Sisupala seems like a lion while the real lion is asleep. But when Lord Krishna speaks, Sisupala will seem like a dog.'

Sisupala completely lost his temper when he heard these words. He rushed up to the old grandfather and waved his sword at him, but the old man stayed calm. He understood that Krishna was something more than he seemed. He knew that there was nothing to fear while Krishna was there.

At last Krishna had heard enough. Sisupala had stopped the most holy ceremony held in India for many hundreds of years, he had been rude to the king and his family and to Krishna himself. Now he was threatening the wise old grandfather with a sword. 'You have said enough and you have done enough. Now there shall be an end to it,' said Krishna.

Krishna aimed at Sisupala with his discus and then hurled the weapon through the air. It flamed as it spun towards Sisupala and then hit him on the head splitting him from head to foot. A great mass of fire burst from the body of the wicked prince. His soul had escaped and was coming towards Krishna. The burning flames bowed towards Krishna as they came near and flickered around his feet. Krishna then took Sisupala's fiery soul into his own body. He had forgiven him his wickedness and brought peace to his anger. And in this way Krishna will save the souls of all people whose minds are full of him, whether they love him or hate him.

The king and his guests were full of joy to know that a god was with them to share the coronation, and the ceremony continued with happiness and rejoicing. King Yudhishthira was crowned the King of Kings of all the earth and the land was rich and contented.

*

In the Bhagavad Gita (The Song of the Blessed Lord) Krishna explains to one of his cousins how Krishna himself is God, and, as God, he is in everything in the universe which he made. Krishna himself is all the other gods. To be saved you must stop thinking selfish thoughts and fill your mind with Krishna. By loving God you will come to understand that the universe is his and you will come to him.

And now listen to my most important word,
Of all my words the most mysterious:
I love you well.
I will tell you how you can be saved.

Keep Me in your mind, love Me and praise Me,
Sacrifice to Me, worship Me:
I promise that you will come to Me
For you are dear to Me.

Forget everything else
And turn to Me, for I am your saviour
And I will keep you
From all evils.

(*from the* Bhagavad Gita 18: 64-66)

*

Duryodhana

The great epic of the Mahabharata tells of the conflict between two sets of cousins for the kingdom of Bharata in the area around Delhi in northern India about 3000 years ago. Although Yudhishthira and his brothers eventually won the losses on both sides were extremely high. Krishna acts as Arjuna's charioteer encouraging and advising him in conversations which are recorded in the Bhagavad Gita (the Song of the Lord) which is one of the most revered pieces of Hindu scripture. Krishna is the eighth incarnation of the great god Vishnu, the Preserver of the universe, who descends to earth to maintain the balance between good and evil until such time as the present cycle of the universe comes to an end. Duryodhana's father ruled in place of his blind elder brother, whose wives and sons, the five brothers, Yudhishthira, Bhima, Arjuna and the twins Nakula and Sadeva, lived in exile with holy men in the forest. On their return Duryodhana lost his rightful claim to the throne and he spent the rest of his life fighting to keep it.

*

Duryodhana's jealousy

Duryodhana was the eldest son of the King of Bharata in Ancient India. He quite expected to rule the land as king when his father died. Until one day there arrived in the city the five sons of Duryodhana's uncle. Duryodhana knew that they had the right to be king before him and his heart felt sick with anger.

His five cousins had lived in the forest all their lives with holy men. Indeed they looked like holy men themselves: their bodies were thin and their clothes were poor but their faces were peaceful and wise. The people of the city grew to love them and cheered as they passed by. Even Duryodhana's father, the King, was happy to keep them at the palace and entertain them at great feasts. But Duryodhana grew cold with hate.

Duryodhana tried to poison one of the brothers, Bhima, but Bhima was as strong as a bull and survived. No-one could prove it was Duryodhana but the brothers were very careful after that. And then he burnt down the house they were asleep in. But they escaped through an underground tunnel to safety in the woods. Duryodhana thought they were all dead until it turned out that they had all married the princess that he had wanted to marry.

Duryodhana planned all sorts of tricks to get rid of his five cousins and tried to get his father to help him. But his father's brothers were wise and loved the five. They made sure that the King listened to common sense. It was finally agreed that the cousins should have half of the land of Bharata and that the eldest of them, Yudhishthira, should be their king.

Everyone was happy as the cousins set out for their new capital city. Even Duryodhana was happy. He knew that the land they had been given was poor land where the people were poor and nothing much grew. And he knew that their new capital city of Indra Prastha was in the middle of a desert.

But the cousins worked hard. They built a palace fit for the gods. They built a city with wide streets and parks and pools and trees and the air was full of the singing of birds. People came from all over India to live in their kingdom and the land grew rich. The crops grew and the cattle were fat and healthy. Yudhisthira became known as the king with no enemies. But that was not quite true.

Duryodhana came to visit his cousins one day in their desert and was amazed to see how they had changed it in to green land where fruit and vegetables grew in plenty. And when he saw the King's magnificent palace he grew blind with jealousy. The walls were white and gold and everywhere was set with pearls and jewels that gleamed in the sunlight. Corridors and stairways were wide and covered with fine soft carpets. The rooms were large and filled with beautiful furniture. Music played, birds sang, sweet flowers filled the air with their perfume.

Duryodhana stepped carefully across a stream of water which crossed one of the rooms and hurt his toe on it. It was made of clear crystal glass and full of beautiful models of fish and water plants. He stepped into a room where the floor shone clear and bright. And fell into the waters of a still pool. And again he walked into a clear glass door and banged his head. The cousins all laughed at the joke, but Duryodhana was furious. His jealousy filled his mind and he could think of nothing else.

Some time later Duryodhana tricked Yudhishthira into a gambling match. By cheating Duryodhana won everything that the cousins had. He had them chased out of the land and they were to remain in the forest for thirteen years. Though they suffered sometimes, they learnt much. But mostly they were happy. After all they were together and had with them their wives and children. At the end of the thirteen years Yudhishthira went back to claim his kingdom.

But Duryodhana was not going to give up so easily. He argued and he shouted and he raged and in the end he challenged the cousins to war. There was nothing else to be done. Throughout the land the kings began to choose sides. Troops were armed and marched to Bharata. The people got ready for a time of suffering and sorrow.

Yudhishthira's brother, Arjuna, was in charge of the army. He paid a visit to another cousin, Krishna. Krishna was the great god Vishnu born on earth and had been a friend and helper of the five brothers for many years. Arjuna knew that Krishna would offer his help in the war that was to come.

But when Arjuna arrived at Krishna's house, there was Duryodhana already talking to Krishna. Of course, Duryodhana was Krishna's cousin too.

'You can't refuse to help me,' said Duryodhana. 'I am your cousin. Fight on my side against the five brothers so that I may keep my Kingdom.'

'I can't fight on either side,' replied Krishna, 'for you are all my cousins. But I cannot refuse you my help either. You can choose between having me on your side but with no weapons or you can have my army of ten thousand warriors fighting for you. In that way I shall be fair to all my cousins.'

Arjuna was quick to answer, 'I choose you,' he said.

'That's fine by me,' laughed Duryodhana. 'I'd rather have ten thousand fighting men on my side.'

'Take them,' replied Krishna, and Duryodhana left without a word of thanks, happy that he had got the best of the deal.

'Why did you choose me?' Krishna asked.

'I shall choose you to drive my chariot,' answered Arjuna, 'and you can encourage me and give me advice. This is more valuable than ten thousand soldiers.'

And the war began. It was bitter and cruel for it was a fight between the members of one family and many many people met their deaths in battle. And as Arjuna had hoped, Krishna proved to be a wise friend always ready to suggest what he should do and full of hope and encouragement. Duryodhana's army fought well and bravely but they were no match for the five brothers. And Duryodhana himself was finally killed in a duel with the mighty Bhima. The five had won.

After months of pain and suffering the land was almost destroyed, many women were widows and many children were orphans. There was sadness and sorrow. But when finally Yudhishthira led his brothers into the capital city the streets were full of joyful people cheering and singing and throwing flowers. Yudhishthira was king of the land of Bharata which he ruled well and with wisdom until his old age many years later.

*

Krishna was no lover of wars and fighting. Before the battle began he went to Duryodhana to beg him not to destroy the land in battle. But Duryodhana was determined to fight and so Krishna had to help defeat him. Most Hindu prayers end with the words 'Peace. Peace. Peace.' Here is the Peace prayer which opens one of the Hindu holy books:

> May God keep us safe;
> May He protect us.
> Let us all work together;
> Let Him enlighten our minds.
> Let us not dislike each other.
> Peace. Peace. Peace.

(*from the* Peace Chant of the Katha Unpanishad *of the* Yajur Veda-Taittiraya)

Nala and Damayanti

Although the main story of the Mahabharata is that of the struggle between the Pandavas and the Kuravas, many other myths and stories are told in the epic. Vyasa, the poet to whom the Mahabharata is attributed, tells the story to King Yudhishthira after the latter had been tricked into a gambling match with his jealous cousin, Duryodhana, and lost everything by his opponent's clever cheating. The King and his brothers were banished to the forest for thirteen years. Vyasa tells the tale to show that there have been those worse off than Yudhishthira and that, by holding fast to their faith, they were ready when the Wheels of Fate turned. Yudhishthira eventually did win his kingdom back.

Nala and Damayanti

At the palace of King Nala in India travelling singers sang of the beauty of Princess Damayanti. They sang so sweetly and so well that the King fell in love with this princess he had never met, and longed to see her.

Many miles away Princess Damayanti heard tales of a king who was handsome and clever and good and the story-teller described him so skilfully that the Princess fell in love with him.

Damayanti could not sleep at night and could not eat her food for thinking about Nala. Her mother and father decided that it was time for their daughter to choose a husband, so a great ceremony was arranged and all the kings and princes of India were invited to come. Damayanti would choose her husband from among them.

But the kings and princes were going to have tough competition. In heaven four gods had heard about the ceremony where the beautiful Damayanti would choose her husband and and they were each determined to be chosen.

The drove their chariots through the sky and came to earth as four handsome princes. As they appeared by the roadside along came Nala on his way to the ceremony.

'Young man,' said Indra, the King of the Gods, 'I guess that you're on your way to Princess Damayanti's husband-choosing ceremony.'

'I am indeed,' replied Nala happily.

'Would you do us a favour?' asked Indra, and as he spoke he shone with glorious light and Nala was amazed.

'Yes, of course,' he said, 'I'll do anything for you.'

'Good,' said Indra, the King of the Gods, 'I'd like you to tell Princess Damayanti how good-looking, kind and intelligent we are so that she will choose one of us to be her husband tomorrow at the ceremony.'

'You must know,' said Nala sadly, 'that I want to marry Damayanti myself. But I promised you a favour and I shall do as you ask.'

There was a flash of light and flower petals fell as the four gods disappeared back to their chariots in the sky.

When Nala saw Damayanti at the palace and gave her the message from the four gods, she thought at first that he was a god for indeed he looked like one. She already knew whom she would pick for her husband the next day.

But when the morning came and the kings and princes lined up for Damayanti to choose, there were five Nalas. The four gods had all appeared as Nala. The Princess looked at each one very hard and at last pointed to the one she thought looked most human. 'I choose this man to be my husband.'

It was the real Nala. The gods were disappointed that they had not been chosen, but were very happy that Nala and Damayanti were together.

King Nala took Damayanti to be his queen in his own country and there they lived happily.

But on their way back to heaven the four gods met the evil god, Kali. Kali was hurrying along in his chariot towards the earth.

'Where are you off to in such a hurry?' asked Indra.

'I'm going to be chosen as Damayanti's husband, of course,' sneered the wicked Kali.

Indra and the gods laughed. 'Well, you're too late. Damayanti has chosen Nala and they are now happily married.'

The four gods flew through the air laughing and Kali's anger began to burn inside him. Nobody saw and nobody knew, but at that moment Kali slipped quietly into Nala's heart determined to destroy him.

That evening Nala played a game of dice as usual. But Kali made him foolish and he began to gamble with more and more money. Each time he lost. The next evening and the next were the same. Nala couldn't stop gambling. Each time he lost. And each time he bet more and more money. Even Damayanti couldn't stop him.

At last Nala lost everything, his money, his fine clothes, his palaces and everything in them, he even lost his throne and his country. All he had left was Damayanti. Sadly and full of shame Nala and Damayanti left the country with nothing but each other.

But Kali's nasty plans were not complete. One night Nala and Damayanti found a little hut to sleep in. During the night Kali's evil was at work in Nala's heart and the King decided that there was no point staying with his wife. He was no good to her. She would do better on her own. And he crept quietly away in the darkness.

Damayanti awoke next morning heart-broken. Now she had nothing at all. She wandered about the country, half mad with sorrow until, after many miles of hard travel and some unpleasant adventures she came back to the palace of her father and mother.

Nala in the meantime had got a job in the stables of a king called Rituparna. He was so good with horses that the King had chosen him to drive his own chariot. They went everywhere together and became great friends.

At Damayanti's palace her parents were very worried. Damayanti spent her days looking pale and unhappy and didn't seem to be interested in anything. Without Nala she did not want to live. They had an idea. Her father would announce that Damayanti was going to have another ceremony to choose another husband. If Nala was still alive anywhere in India, he would be sure to come. The messengers were sent far and wide.

King Rituparna heard about the ceremony and called Nala to him. 'We're rather late,' said Rituparna. 'If you can drive me to the ceremony in time, I'll give you whatever you want.'

'Teach me how to gamble as cleverly as you do,' said Nala.

'Anything you like,' replied the King, 'But hurry up.'

Nala whipped up the horses and drove like the wind to the palace of Damayanti's parents. As soon as Nala and Damayanti saw each other they were happy together again. Damayanti's parents were delighted and even King Rituparna was glad to see two people so full of joy and love. He taught Nala all about gambling before he left and Nala thanked him many times.

Together Nala and Damayanti set off for Nala's kingdom which he won back in just one throw of the dice. As king and queen they ruled the land in peace and happiness for many years.

*

The flame of a lamp, although it may be small,
destroys immense darkness.
In the same way, knowledge, although it may be
small, will destroy great ignorance.

(*from the* Atmaprabodha Unpanishad 41:28-29 *of the* Rig Veda)

*

He is Brahma: He is Shiva; He is Indra;
He is the Never-Changing, the Rule over all;
He is Vishnu;
He is Life; He is Time;
He is Fire; He is the Moon;
He alone is everything, what has been and what will be;
He is the Everlasting.
By knowing Him you can live forever:
There is no other way to be saved.

(*from the* Kaivalya Upanishad 12:8-9 *of the* Yajur Veda — Taittiriya)

*

Yudhishthira

The story of Yudhishthira and his four brothers is told in the vast Hindu epic, the Mahabharata. It deals with the conflict between the sons of King Pandu and those of his brother, King Dhritarashtra Kuru. Pandu's sons, though legally his, are in fact the children of various gods, Yudhishthira being the son of the god Dharma, God of Righteousness. The Great Sacrifice in this story is not the same event as in the previous story. That took place at the beginning of the King's reign; this took place towards the end. The sacrifice actually involved the ritual killing and eating of a sacred horse which had been set free and followed through the lands over which Yudhishthira was sovereign. The submission of the local king was accepted and the horse continued its journey until it returned to the capital city. The sacrifice entailed the giving away of large sums of money and other gifts and its purpose was to purify the king of grief and sin for the next world and to ensure the properity and well-being of the kingdom. The events on which the Mahabharata is based are believed to have taken place at some time before 1000 BCE in the area around Delhi.

*

King Yudhishthira and the mongoose's story

King Yudhishthira was the great king of all India. His life had been long and full of adventures and now he ruled the land wisely and well. He decided that the time had come for him to perform the Great Sacrifice.

He called his priests and the high priest of them all and they began to prepare him for the great occasion. Hymns were sung and the King said prayers and learned how the Great Sacrifice should be carried out.

The day of the Sacrifice came. Kings and queens from many lands had arrived to bow before the great Yudhishthira. The princes, wise men, and priests were all there.

On the first day presents of food were made to all who had come and they were all well pleased. Then the place of Sacrifice was prepared by many priests who followed exactly the books of the scriptures. All was ready.

On the second day the King entered the place of the Sacrifice dressed in his most magnificent clothes and wearing his most dazzling jewels. His chariot was pulled by the finest horses in India and his family followed in a glorious procession before the guests from many lands. Gifts of animals were given to the gods, their meat was roasted and eaten by the people in a wonderful feast and everyone went to bed full and happy.

The third day King Yudhishthira was washed with holy water and was proclaimed king of the whole world by all the other kings and queens, by the princes and lords and ladies, by the priests and by all the people. And then the King gave presents of money and food and jewellery and ornaments and clothes to everyone who was there and not one person was unhappy with what he got. There was music and dancing, singing and laughing, sweet smells and sweet sounds and happiness everywhere, for everyone knew that the land would be well because of the Great Sacrifice. And the people went home full of gladness and King Yudhishthira was very contented.

But when the place was cleared and only a few priests remained, a mongoose appeared. Half of his body was made of gold. He spoke to the priests in a deep low voice and they all stopped to listen.

'This sacrifice may have been great,' said the mongoose, 'but it is not so great as a handful of flour.

'I shall tell you how it was that a handful of flour took a man to heaven and how it was that my coat is half gold.

'I used to live in a hole near a priest's house. He lived there with his wife and his son and his son's wife. They were holy people and good who spent all their time praising God. They never cared about owning things and only ate just enough to keep themselves alive.

'After the farmers had gathered in their harvest the priest's family would go out into the fields and collect any grains that had been left. They ground the grain into flour and this would last them until the next harvest if they ate only a small handful once a day.

'And then there came a drought. No rain fell that year and the plants withered and died. The farmers sowed their seeds but nothing would grow. There was hunger throughout the land. The priest and his family had hardly anything to eat.

'One day after the priest and his family had said their prayers and worshipped God, they shared among them the last of the flour. It was only a tiny handful each. But before they had chance to start eating a visitor came to their hut. Gladly they welcomed him in.

'But what could the priest give him to eat. They had nothing. The priest gave him the small handful of flour that he had been going to eat himself.

'The guest was still hungry. He had travelled a long way and needed more than a handful of flour. The priest's wife gave her flour to the hungry man.

'But still the guest was hungry. The priest's son and his wife also gave away their flour. The family now had no flour left to share. They had nothing. Their visitor ate the last of the food. And as he did he seemed to grow in size. Light glowed from his body and the tiny dark hut was lit by pure shining light.

'It was indeed the god, Yama. "You had very little to give," said Yama, "and yet you gave all that you had. The door of heaven is hard to open and it is being greedy that keeps it shut for most people. You have given away the only thing that belonged to you. For you the door of heaven has been opened and the gods are singing songs of joy.

'The god led the family from their poor hut to where a golden chariot waited. Singing could be heard from above and sweet-smelling flowers were falling to the ground from the skies. The priest and his family climbed aboard and the god drove the chariot higher and higher through the clouds until they all entered the heaven of the righteous and the good.

'And I peeped out of my hole,' said the mongoose, 'as the flowers from heaven fell. And I came half out of my hole to breathe in the sweet smell. As I did, half of my fur was turned to gold.

'And now I go from place to place where there are good and holy people to see if I can change the rest of my coat to gold. I have been to lonely places in the forests where holy men pray, I have been to the palaces of kings and I have waited in temples, but as you see, my coat is still the same. I came here to this Great Sacrifice where the good King Yudhishthira was giving many things away to many people. But the other half of my coat has not turned to gold. And so you see, the King may have been kind and generous and the sacrifice may have been great, but it is not so great as a handful of flour.'

The mongoose whose coat was half gold turned from the priests in the place of Sacrifice and continued his journey.

*

Come to God in the proper way,
  with a peaceful mind and calmly,
and truly you will learn about God
  and know that the Everliving God is Truth.

(*from the* Mundaka Unpanishad 1,2:13 *of the* Atharva-Veda)

This is the truth:
  From a blazing fire come many thousands of sparks;
  from the Unchanging God come many kinds of beings;
  and to Him they return.

  God is holy and has no shape;
  He is inside everything and all around everywhere;
  He is pure and higher than anything,
  the Unchanging God.

(*from the* Mundaka Upanishad 2,1:1-2)

*

King Yudhishthira goes to Heaven

King Yudhishthira had fought for many years to defeat his wicked cousin and win back the land for himself. And when Yudhishthira became king he ruled the land fairly and there was peace once more. But there came a time when the King and his faithful brothers wanted to discover the truth about life, and to understand the mystery of God. They gave away their jewels and their beautiful clothes, and they gave away all their riches. And, wearing only the clothes of holy men King Yudhishthira set off with his wife Draupadi, and his brothers, Bhima and Arjuna, and the twins Nakula and Sadeva.

The people of the city came with them to the edge of the forest and begged them to stay, but, with a last wave, they set off on their journey of truth. Tagging along with them was their little brown dog.

Across rivers and deserts they went, over hills and through forests, until they started to climb the lower hills of the mighty Himalaya mountains. Up and up they went, the King, his wife, the brothers and the small brown dog. And one by one they began to fall.

First the King's wife collapsed and died. The travelling had been too hard. But the party carried on. Then Sadeva and sometime later his twin, who could not go on without him collapsed. And Bhima fell. Yudhishthira tired and thirsty and longing for rest carried on upwards, his dog beside him.

All at once there was a great thundering rumble and a flash of lightning. Indra, the King of the gods, appeared in his chariot.

'Get in,' commanded the god. 'I have come to take you to heaven.'

'I can't leave without my wife and my brothers who have fallen further back,' answered Yudhishthira. 'I cannot leave them behind.'

'You will find that they are in heaven already,' said Indra. 'Get in.'

Yudhishthira began to climb up on to the chariot bringing his dog with him.

'There is no room in heaven for dogs,' said Indra. 'You can come, but the dog must stay.'

'But this dog has been my faithful friend throughout the journey. I am his protector,' said Yudhishthira.

'I am offering you heaven,' said Indra, 'and you are fussing about a dog.'

'All living things are important,' replied the King, 'and this dog especially. If he cannot come into heaven, then I will not either.'

When King Yudhishthira had finished speaking the desert air began to glow with a great shining light. His small brown dog changed into Dharma, the God of Righteousness.

'You have proved that you are indeed fit to go into heaven,' Dharma's voice boomed across the sands. 'You are a man who is faithful to his friends and who loves all living creatures. Come with us.'

Indra and Dharma took the King higher and higher and the whole sky blazed with their glory. As they entered heaven the gods and holy men welcomed Yudhishthira with open arms and smiling faces. Flower petals fell and music was heard and all was happiness.

But when Yudhishthira looked around he saw, sitting on a magnificent throne, his wicked cousin, the cousin who had stolen his land.

'I am not staying here with my evil cousin,' said Yudhishthira. 'Take me to my wife and brothers.'

'Go there if you must,' said Indra, 'But this is where heaven is.'

A messenger led Yudhisthira along a path. The path grew narrow and steep and finally plunged into an underground cave. Now the path was slippery with blood and the air was filled with a foul smell and cries of pain echoed around the King. Maggots dripped from the roof and stinging flies bit at him as he walked. They passed by a steaming evil river. Human skulls lay on the banks. The King could hardly breathe for the choking smoke.

In the darkness a voice called out, 'Stay. Stay. As you passed we could smell sweet fresh air. Stay here for a while.'

Through the gloom Yudhishthira's eyes could make out his wife and brothers lying in pain on the boiling rocks. The King sent the messenger back. 'You can tell Indra,' he said angrily, 'that I shall stay in this hell with those I love. If I can bring them some happiness in this awful place, then this is where I will stay.'

The darkness disappeared as a clear sun rose. The cave, the rocks, the river and the cries of pain vanished. Yudishthira was with his family in heaven.

'This has been your last test,' said Dharma. 'You are better fitted for heaven than anyone here. There shall be no more hate and no more struggling for you. Happiness is yours for ever.'

*

Most people do not have the strength that King Yudhishthira showed. Most people need to put their trust in God to help them through difficult times. Here is a hymn by the 17th century CE poet, Tukaram. He worshipped God as Vishnu, but Hindus believe all gods to be One.

Who else asks if we are tired and weary?
Who else but you, O Lord?

Who else can we tell we are happy or sad?
Who else can cure our thirst?

Who can cure our illness?
Who can carry us safely across the angry sea?

Who will give us what we want in our hearts?
And who will hold us to his loving heart?

What other master can we have?
What other helper is there?

O Lord, you know all things.
I bow at your feet.

(Pandurang *by Tukaram*)

*

Rama

Rama is the seventh incarnation of the god, Vishnu the Preserver of the Universe, who was born as a prince in northern India and whose mission it was to destroy the evil power of the demon, Ravana. The story of this incarnation is told in the epic Ramayana. Vishnu is generally believed to have ten incarnations, although many Hindus worship the Supreme Being as Vishnu or one of his forms and hold that his incarnations are innumerable. In this story Rama appears to the poor farmer to maintain the balance in favour of good against evil in his role as Preserver.

*

Rama and the poor farmer

There lived in India a poor farmer who was always in debt to a very mean money-lender. When the harvests were bad, the farmer had to borrow money to buy seed to plant for the next year. When the harvests were good, the farmer had to pay the money-lender back much more than he owed him. So the farmer worked hard and struggled to live, while the money-lender grew richer and richer for doing nothing.

One day the farmer begged the money-lender to tell him the secret of his wealth. 'It wouldn't hurt you to tell me,' said the farmer. 'I only want enough money to live by.'

The money-lender put on a holy voice like a priest's and said, 'You must ask Rama, our God. God gives everything in this world. Ask the Lord Rama if you could have some money.'

The poor farmer set off in search of Rama, taking with him three small loaves of bread for the journey.

Soon he met a priest coming along the road. 'Excuse me, priest,' said the farmer, 'can you help me. please? I'm looking for Rama.'

The farmer gave the priest one of the loaves. The priest ate it, smiled, but said nothing and carried on his way.

A holy man came along the road. 'Please, holy man,' said the poor farmer, 'I'm looking for Rama, Can you help me?'

He gave the holy man a loaf. The holy man ate it, smiled, but, saying nothing, went off down the road.

A poor man came along. It didn't really look as though he would know anything about Lord Rama, but the farmer offered him his last loaf, saying 'I'm looking for Rama. I don't suppose you could help me, could you?'

'But, of course,' laughed the poor man. 'I am Rama. How can I help you?'

The farmer told him his story, how he worked hard and struggled to live, while the money-lender took nearly everything he had. 'I don't want much,' said the farmer, 'but a little something would help.'

Rama felt sorry for the poor hard-working farmer and gave him a conch shell, the type they blow in Hindu temples. He showed him a special way to blow this shell to get a deep booming note out of it. 'You can wish for anything you want,' said Rama, 'but be especially careful of the money-lender. He's mean and nasty, but he's certainly clever too.'

The farmer thanked Rama many times and rushed back to his home. As he entered the village the money-lender realised that he must have had some good luck, and wandered over to the farmer's house. He was so cunning and clever with words that the farmer soon found that he had told the money-lender all about meeting Rama and all about the magic conch shell.

And while the poor farmer slept, the wicked money-lender crept into his house and stole it out of his hand. He dashed home with it and blew. But not a note came from it. He blew this way and that. He blew until his cheeks nearly burst. But nothing.

Next morning he went to the farmer and admitted stealing the shell. 'But I can't use it, because I don't know how,' said the money-lender, 'and you can't use it because you haven't got it.'

Sadly the farmer agreed to a deal. The money-lender would give him the conch shell to blow any time he wanted it. But whatever he wished for, he had to wish for two of them for the money-lender.

The farmer never asked for much, but it did upset him to see that the money-lender always had twice as much. There came a time of drought, when no rain fell and the rivers and even the wells began to dry up. The farmer wished for a deep well. Immediately two wells also appeared at the money-lender's house. The farmer had had enough. He suddenly had a brainwave. The farmer wished that one of his eyes should go blind. Immediately both of the money-lender's eyes went blind. He stumbled about unable to see and fell into one of his wells and drowned.

The farmer lived happily and never wished for much. But he always praised Rama for the gift he had given him.

*

Hindus see God in many shapes and forms. Many Hindus worship God as Rama, and many hymns have been written praising Him. Tulsi Das was a poet who lived about 400 years ago. All of his work was written in praise of Rama.

Great King, who gives comfort to your servants,
  Rama, I give myself to you.
Great King, beautiful and good,
  Rama, I give myself to you.
Great King, who makes all pain and sorrow disappear,
  Rama, I give myself to you.
Great King, with the kind eyes,
  Rama, I give myself to you.
I give myself to Rama, who is kind and merciful,
  Who protects the humble, who drives away sin.
I give myself to Rama, to his safety,
  to keep me free from the wickedness of the world.

(*from* Kavitavali 7: 111 *by Tulsi Das*)

*

Durga

Durga, the Inaccessible Goddess, is an aspect of the wife of Shiva, one of the three great gods of Hinduism. As Parvati, goddess of the Earth, she is a beautiful young woman and the counterpart of Shiva, but she took on the aspect of Durga at the gods' request to defeat a demon, Mahesasura, who had dethroned them all. Her ten hands carry weapons given by the gods and, though beautiful, her face has a terrifying serenity. Riding a lion she attacked the demon, who, despite many changes of form, was unable to escape the thrust of her deadly lance.

*

Durga and the gift of money or happiness

There lived in India a young man called Yashovarman who was the servant of a king. The king, however, never gave Yashovarman anything. Yashovarman saw expensive things every day and worked among the richest people in the land, but he never had anything to call his own. Yashovarman became more and more miserable, until finally he left the king's court.

Yashovarman travelled to the mountains where stood a temple of the goddess, Durga. He threw himself on the floor before her statue, saying, 'I shall lie here and pray to the goddess until she grants me a wish. If she grants me a wish I shall ask for a fortune in money and then I shall be happy. If I die here, I shall be better off dead than poor and miserable.'

And so Yashovarman lay before the statue of Durga praying with all his might. For many days he lay there and took no food. He did not move a muscle but lay perfectly still praying to the goddess.

And the goddess looked upon him kindly and appeared to him in a dream in all her glory. She appeared to him as she was when she had fought against a dreadful demon who had beaten the gods in battle. Her face was proud and calm and glowed with light; she had ten arms and each hand carried a fearsome weapon; she was riding a great lion. She was so powerful that Yashovarman tried to wake himself out of his bad dream, but the goddess would not let him.

She spoke to him in a voice that seemed to shake the mountains and fill the sky: 'Yashovarman,' she said, 'I will grant you a wish. You can choose between money or happiness.'

'There's no difference,' said Yashovarman. 'If you have money, then you'll be happy. You have to have money to be happy.'

'Before you choose,' said Durga, 'you must find out the difference. Go back to your own land and I will lead you to the homes of two merchants. When you have seen them, you may choose between money and happiness.'

And so Yashovarman went down from the mountains and back to his own land. And when he came back to his own city he met a merchant called Arthavarman. The merchant took Yashovarman back to his house and Yashovarman was amazed by the riches he saw there. Everything in the house was expensive and beautiful. Gold and jewels were everywhere. The furniture was soft and comfortable, the walls were wonderfully decorated, and there were servants ready to bring anything Artharvarman could want. When it was time for the evening meal the table was covered with all the most delicious foods that could be imagined, and Yashovarman enjoyed a very hearty meal. The merchant Arthavarman hardly ate anything.

'Why aren't you eating?' asked Yashovarman in surprise. 'There are all sorts of lovely things here.'

'Oh, I can't each much,' said the merchant. 'I've got a bad stomach and I don't really enjoy my food.' And the merchant's face was pale and covered all over with worry lines.

That night Yashovarman heard the merchant wake up screaming. He had dreadful stomach ache and had had bad dreams. He was violently sick and could not get back to sleep again. In the morning his face was paler than ever and he looked thoroughly unhappy as he set off to work to earn even more money for himself.

'Well, there wasn't much fun at that house,' thought Yashovarman. 'He had all the money I could wish for, but he certainly wasn't happy.'

Yashovarman then called at the house of a merchant called Bhogavarman. Bhogavarman's house was nice, but it was not so full of rich things as the first merchant's house had been. And when the evening meal was served, there was not quite so much of it and it wasn't quite such good food. But Bhogavarman was very different from the first merchant. He chatted away happily while he tucked into a very enjoyable meal. And when the food was eaten and the wine was drunk Yashovarman and Bhogavarman went to bed and slept soundly and peacefully until they both woke refreshed and happy the next morning.

Leaving the city, Yashovarman travelled up to the mountain temple of the goddess Durga. And there he prayed that he might be granted happiness rather than money, for you can be happy and yet have no money at all, but however much money you have, you cannot buy happiness.

Durga gave Yashovarman his wish and he lived a happy peaceful and long life.

*

For many religious people true happiness can only be found by having faith in God.

The learned scholar lies awake at night
  with his mind confused by knowing too much;
The greedy man cannot sleep for thinking about
  land and money and houses;
Others lie awake worrying about enjoying themselves
or dying or being ill;
But I sleep soundly —
  my faith is in God.

(*from* Kavitavali 7: 109 *by Tulsi Das*)

*

The Jews

Samson of Dan

After Moses had led the Israelites from slavery in Egypt they settled according to tribal allocations in the land of Canaan (parts of modern Israel, Jordan, Lebanon and Syria). They were not united and there was often friction between the Israelites and the other peoples of the area. From time to time a 'judge' would arise, a military and political leader of such standing that he or she commanded respect and spoke with authority thereafter. Twelve such are mentioned in the Book Judges, of which Samson of the tribe of Dan is the last. The tribe of Dan held land to the east of Joppa (now Jaffa, Israel) and were often in conflict with the Philistines, invaders from the Aegean who held territory along the Mediterranean coast around Gaza (Egypt). During his lifetime (c.1000 BCE) Samson held the Philistines in check, but eventually the tribe of Dan was forced to move to the north of Lake Galilee.

*

Samson and the lion riddle

Samson belonged to the Israelite tribe of Dan. The Danites lived always in danger from the Philistine people of the neighbouring country. There were often arguments and fights, and sometimes there were battles between the Israelites and the Philistines. But Samson became famous throughout Israel because he protected his people from the attacks of the Philistines.

*

Imagine his parents' horror when Samson told them he wanted to marry a Philistine girl! Samson was on his way one day to see the girl in the village of Timnah where she lived. As he was passing the vineyards a young lion suddenly sprang out at him. Samson had no weapons and so he fought the lion with his bare hands. He tore the lion to pieces! and carried on to Timnah. Some weeks later Samson came past the vineyards on his way to marry the Philistine girl and he stopped to look what had happened to the lion's body. A swarm of bees had made a nest in it and Samson put in his hand and tasted the honey.

During the wedding feast in Timnah there was a game of riddles. Samson said, 'If anyone can guess the answer to my riddle before the end of the week I shall give him thirty sets of clothes. If no-one guesses the answer then you Philistines must give me thirty sets of clothes.'

The Philistines liked a good guessing game. 'Out of the eater came something to eat. Out of the strong came something sweet,' said Samson smiling, for who could possibly guess what he had seen.

After three days the Philistines were cross. No-one had any idea of the answer. They went to Samson's wife and threatened her: 'If we have to pay Samson thirty sets of clothes we'll be ruined. Find out the answer or we'll burn your house and you in it.'

But Samson would say nothing. On the fifth and sixth day still no answer. On the seventh day Samson grew so tired of hearing his wife pestering and weeping that he told her the story of the lion. And so when Samson told his riddle on the last day of the week one of the Philistines was able to answer him: 'What is sweeter than honey? What is stronger than a lion?'

Realising that he had been tricked and that he now owed the Philistines thirty sets of clothes, Samson lost his temper. He stormed out of the house, went down to next Philistine village and killed thirty men. He brought back their clothes, flung them at the Philistines, then went back home leaving his new wife in Timnah.

Some months went by and Samson decided to visit his wife in Timnah only to find that her father had married her to someone else. Again Samson was angry. He went out into the field and caught three hundred foxes which he tied in pairs tail to tail. Then he set fire to their tails and let the foxes ran about burning the corn and the vineyards and the orchards as well.

The Philistines in Timnah swore to get their own back. Samson was nowhere to be seen so a gang of them went to his wife's house and burned the house and her in it. Samson suddenly appeared from nowhere crying out for revenge. He attacked the Philistines and many were hurt and many were killed. It was some time before they caused any more trouble.

*

Samson and Delilah

The Philistines had tried many times to capture Samson the Israelite, but he was so strong that he had killed hundreds of them in battle and they were afraid of him. When the Philistine leaders heard that Samson had fallen in love with a Philistine woman called Delilah, they went to see her. 'We will give you eleven hundred silver coins if you can find out the secret of Samson's great strength,' they said.

So Delilah asked Samson, 'Tell me the secret of your great strength and how you could be captured and held.'

'If they tied me up with seven new bow-strings, I should be as weak as anyone else.' Delilah tied Samson with seven new bow-strings, then signalled to a gang of Philistines who were hiding in the next room. 'The Philistines are here!' she called out. But Samson just snapped the bow-strings and laughed. The Philistines stayed hidden.

'You're teasing me,' said Delilah. 'Tell me the real secret of your strength.'

'I can only be held down with new rope,' said Samson, 'then I should be as weak as anyone else.' Delilah fetched a brand new rope and tightly bound Samson's arms and legs. 'The Philistines are here!' called out Delilah. Samson stood up and snapped the rope as if it were cotton and the Philistines stayed in hiding.

'It's getting late, Samson, and you are still teasing me. Please tell me the truth of your great strength.' 'You must weave seven locks of my hair in a loom and peg it down,' replied Samson sleepily. Delilah weaved his hair tightly and pegged it firmly, and when he was asleep and the Philistines were ready once more, Delilah woke him shouting, 'The Philistines are here!' As Samson woke he sat up and the peg was simply pulled out. Quietly, but quickly, the Philistines crept away.

From then on, day after day, Delilah tried to find out the secret of Samson's strength. 'You can't really love me, she said, 'or you would tell me the truth.' At last Samson grew tired of hearing her and finally blurted out the truth: 'The secret of my strength is in my long hair. I have never had it cut. If my head was shaved I should be as weak as anyone else.'

That night the Philistines were again in hiding in the next room. As Samson slept a barber came and cut his long hair short to the scalp. 'The Philistines are here!' called Delilah, and Samson awoke. As the Philistines rushed in Samson prepared to fight, but he was as weak as anyone else and he was outnumbered. He was tied and bound and they gouged out his eyes. Hurt and bleeding Samson was dragged off to the Philistine prison leaving Delilah happily counting her eleven hundred silver coins.

Many months later a great feast was held in the temple of the Philistines. There was singing and eating and drinking and dancing and, as a special entertainment, Samson was to be brought in to amuse the people. As the Philistines' great enemy staggered in, bound in chains and unable to see, none of the laughing, jeering crowd noticed that his hair had been growing while he was in prison. All the lords and their ladies were there and people pushed and crowded to get a good view. There were hundreds of people on the temple roof.

As Samson stumbled along towards the temple, he prayed to God, 'Lord, remember me. Give me strength for one last time.' Samson was led to the centre of the temple where he put his left and his right arms round the two stone pillars which supported the whole building. With a roar of anger he tightened his muscles and shouted, 'Let me die with the Philistines!' Then he summoned up all his strength and leaned forward pulling the two stone pillars with him. The whole temple collapsed and the Philistines, lords and peasants alike, were killed by the falling stones. It is said that, as he died, Samson killed more Philistines than he had killed during his life.

The fact that Samson's strength, which came from God, enabled him to defeat the enemies of Israel was considered right and proper by the Israelites. They maintained their faith in one true God while their enemies, in this case the Philistines, worshipped false idols. There is a great variety of feeling expressed in the Psalms, the collection of hymns used in the Temple in Jerusalem. Psalm 9 is attributed to King David and matches the feeling of the story of Samson although it was written long after his time.

> I thank you, Lord with all my heart;
> I will tell all the marvellous things You've done.
> I am happy and joyful in You,
> I will sing praise to Your name, Highest God.
> All my enemies run away,
> they fall and die before You,
> for You are the good Judge on Your throne,
> You are on my side and support what I believe in.
> You have spoken to the people and destroyed the wicked,
> You have wiped out their names for ever.
> Our enemies are finished, their cities are in ruins
> and no-one will ever remember them.
> But the Lord is King for ever.

(*from* Psalm 9:1-7)

*

King Solomon

Solomon (born c.986 BCE ruled c.972-c.932) consolidated the military gains his father David had made by political alliances and the development of a strong army and navy. Much of his wealth came from natural resources as well as from excise levied on the camel caravans travelling the trade route through Israel. Apart from slave labour, using prisoners of war, King Solomon imposed conscription on thirty thousand of his own people who worked one month in three often in foreign countries, or to build the defences of Jerusalem as well as the royal palace and the Temple. His unpopularity because of this led to the downfall of his house after his death. Fabled for his wisdom, Solomon is supposed to have written the Books of Proverbs, Ecclesiastes and the Song of Songs to be found in the Bible.

*

King Solomon the Wise

King David ruled the prople of Israel wisely for forty years, and during his time the people worshipped the one God faithfully as did David. Before he died he passed the crown to his son Solomon and told him to obey the laws that God had given to the prophet Moses many years before.

Not long after he became king, Solomon had a dream in which God spoke to him. 'What would you like me to give you?' asked God.

In his dream Solomon answered, 'My father, David, worshipped you faithfully and you looked after him. I am only a young man not used to running a country. So all I ask is that you will give me a heart that can tell the difference between right and wrong so that I can rule your people wisely.'

God was pleased with Solomon: 'You could have asked me for anything: for long life, for riches, for revenge on your enemies, but you have asked for a heart that can tell the difference between right and wrong, and that I shall give you. But I shall also give you what you did not ask for: you shall be rich and have greater glory than any king. And you shall have a long life, if you obey my laws as your father David obeyed my laws.

King Solomon woke up and went back to Jerusalem where he worshipped God, then gave a great feast for all his servants.

Indeed King Solomon became famous as the wisest of kings, and if ever anyone wanted a problem sorting out or an argument settled, they brought it to the King.

One day Solomon was seated on his great gold throne when two women were led in to stand at the bottom of the steps. The two women lived in the same house and had given birth to babies at the same time. One of the babies had died and the first woman claimed that the other had swopped them over giving her the dead child. They shouted and they argued in front of the King. Solomon thought, one woman says that her child is alive and the other's is dead; while the second woman says that the other's is dead and hers is alive. 'Bring me a sword,' he called to one of his soldiers, 'and cut the living baby in two. The women can have half each.'

The second woman said, 'That's fair. If I can't have the baby alive, neither of us should have it.'

But the first woman shouted in fear, 'My lord, give her the baby, but whatever you do, don't kill it.'

'Give the baby to this woman,' said the King, 'for the baby is obviously hers.'

Everyone who heard about the case agreed that Solomon had the wisdom of God within him.

*

There was peace with other countries in King Solomon's time and the land became rich and prosperous. The King had a strong army of chariots and a large navy; his ships traded with countries all over the world and brought back many treasures. And Solomon wanted Jerusalem to look like the capital city of a powerful king, so he set to work finishing the city walls and had plans for a palace for himself and a temple for God. Thousands of slaves were used and thousands of ordinary people were made to leave their homes and jobs for one month out of every three to come and work for the King. It took thirteen years of back-breaking work and Solomon's enormous and truly magnificent palace was finished.

The King's unhappy workers were also busy building the Temple on a hill to the north of the city, near to the palace. It only took half the time to build that the palace had taken; and it was only half as big as the palace, not quite as tall, but it too was a wonderful building. There were great open courtyards and two huge halls and the whole place was lit by large gold lamps which shone on the golden carvings and on the gold of the walls, ceiling and floors, for Solomon had the entire Temple plated with gold.

In the heart of the Temple was a room called the Holy of Holies. No-one was ever allowed to enter this room except the High Priest who went in only once a year. This room was entirely of gold. On the back wall were the statues of two angels, more than twice as big as a tall man, with their wings stretched out. But the most important thing in the room was a wooden chest; the Ark of the Covenant. In the Ark were two flat stones on which were the words of the law God had given to Moses in the desert hundreds of years before. The first of these laws of God reads: 'You shall have no other gods but God.'

*

King Solomon ruled for forty years and during his time many people became rich and lived very comfortable lives. Many people were forced to do work they did not want to do, building for the King. Inside his beautiful palace Solomon lived a life of great luxury. He had as much of anything as anyone could want, including wives. He had married a thousand wives from countries all over the world. His wives worshipped many different gods and so Solomon built temples for them to worship their own gods in their own way. As time went by Solomon himself began to join in worshipping these other gods and began to forget about the one God his father David had worshipped.

The King had promoted a man called Jeroboam to be in charge of the hundreds of workers building the walls of the city. As Jeroboam was out walking one day the prophet Ahijah stoped him. Ahijah pulled off his cloak and tore it into twelve strips. 'My cloak is Israel,' said Ahijah, 'and this is the way it will be torn apart.'

Ahijah gave ten of the strips to Jeroboam and held up the two that were left. 'After the death of King Solomon you shall rule over ten parts of the land, while Solomon's son will have only these two parts. For the King has stopped worshipping God as he should and has been praying to the false gods of his wives.'

The King found out about the words of the prophet Ahijah and Jeroboam had to flee to Egypt until King Solomon died. And it happened as the prophet said. When the people realised that they were going to have to work just as hard building palaces and fortresses for Solomon's son as they had for Solomon, they chased his son out of Israel and chose Jeroboam to be their new king.

*

King Solomon is famous for having been an extremely wise man. He made a collection of hundreds of sensible sayings called proverbs, some of which were surely made up by the King himself:

God's name is like a strong castle:
good people can run there and be safe.
(*from the* Book of Proverbs 18:10)

The eyes of God are everywhere,
watching the evil and the good people. (*from* 15:3)

God hates liars;
He loves people who tell the truth. (*from* 12:22)

Fools lose their temper when they are angry;
sensible people wait and calm down. (*from* 29:11)

If you answer people gently they won't get angry;
but sharp words stir up anger. (*from* 15:1)

It's better to have only a little, and love God
than to have treasure, and trouble following you. (*from* 15:16)

It's better to have only a dry piece of bread to eat in peace
than to have a feast in a house full of arguing. (*from* 17:1)

Fools always think they are right;
sensible people listen to advice. (*from* 12:15)

Fools believe everything they hear;
sensible people are careful how they go.   *(from 14:15)*

Only fools make fun of other people;
sensible people keep quiet.   *(from 11:12)*

Don't give stupid people stupid answers
or you too will become stupid.   *(from 26:4)*

If you are cruel to the poor, you insult God who made you;
be generous to the poor and honour God.   *(from 14:31)*

If you shut your ears when people cry for help,
when you cry for help, no-one will hear you.   *(from 21:13)*

If you are kind to poor people, it's like lending to God;
God will pay you back.   *(from 19:17)*

Don't boast about what you're going to do tomorrow;
you don't even know what will happen today.   *(from 27:1)*

Elijah

The prophet Elijah lived during the reign of King Ahab of Israel (874-853 BCE). At this time the Jewish people lived in two separate kingdoms, Judah to the south and Israel to the north. The chronicles relating to these times were written from the southern point of view and emphasise the fact that while the southern people remained faithful to the Jerusalem Temple and to the covenant with God, the northerners set up shrines of their own and even indulged in worshipping gods imported from neighbouring countries. Ahab seems to have been a strong political and military leader; archaeological evidence bears witness to this, but he is criticised by Elijah for not only having neglected the true Jewish faith, but for allowing and encouraging his queen Jezebel in her worship of the Phoenician gods. Jezebel became for later biblical writers a symbol of absolute wickedness.

The story of Elijah's transportation into heaven by means of a fiery chariot developed into a belief that Elijah would one day return. The prophet Malachi wrote that God would send Elijah to reform the people before the Day of Judgement, and Jews to this day leave a place empty at their table during the Feast of the Passover with food and wine for the prophet, should he return.

*

Elijah and the priests of Baal

Ahab was the King of Israel over a thousand years ago. He was strong in battle and had a great army, he built fortresses and castles to protect his people, and during his time the country grew rich. King Ahab's own palace was beautiful and luxurious. Precious ivory was used everywhere as decoration as were precious stones and gold and silver. But Ahab was not strong in his belief in the one God of Israel. He often worshipped statues of foreign gods brought to Israel by his wife, the wicked Queen Jezebel.

Jezebel was a princess of Phoenicia where many gods were worshipped. She brought with her to Israel statues of them and even had a temple made to the god Baal in the palace courtyard. Statues were put on the hills of the country and the priests of Baal prayed to them. If any of the Jewish priests complained, Queen Jezebel sent the King's soldiers to kill them.

It happened that there was drought in the land of Israel. The rains did not come and the crops died and the rivers ran dry. Queen Jezebel and her priests prayed to their gods, especially to Baal whom they called the Rain God. But no rain came.

God spoke to the prophet Elijah and told him to go to the King. 'So you're the one causing trouble in Israel,' said King Ahab. But Elijah was not afraid of the King. He faced him bravely and said, 'It is you and your family who are causing trouble in the land. You have given up the one true God and you worship statues of foreign gods.'

The King was troubled and made no answer to the prophet Elijah.

'Call all the people of Israel to Mount Carmel,' commanded Elijah. 'Bring there also the four hundred priests of Baal, servants of your Queen Jezebel.' And the King did as Elijah ordered.

The next morning as the sun rose over the dry and thirsty land the people and the priests of Baal were gathered on Mount Carmel. Elijah spoke in a loud voice: 'The time has come to choose. If the Lord is God, you must follow him. If Jezebel's rain-god, Baal is God, you must follow him. I am the only prophet of the Lord God here, and I stand against four hundred priests of Baal. Let us see whose God will answer our prayers.'

The people grew silent as the priests of Baal built a stone altar and lay on it the body of a bull as a sacrifice. But no fire was lit to burn the bull. The priests of Baal must pray to their god to light the sacrifice himself. The four hundred priests began. They cast spells and sang magical songs. They danced a strange hobbling dance round the altar. They prayed and shouted and they beat themselves with swords, but the bull on the altar did not burn.

Elijah laughed. 'Has Baal gone for a walk? Is he busy? Perhaps he's asleep. Shout louder and you might wake him up!'

But midday came and the priests of Baal had still not managed to light their sacrifice by praying. Now it was Elijah's turn. 'Fill four large jars,' said the prophet, 'and pour water over the bull, the wood and the altar.' This was done. 'Do it a second time. And a third.' The scarifice was soaked and the water ran down the sides of the altar and wet the ground round about.

Elijah prayed aloud to God: 'Oh Lord, I have done as you told me. Show the people that you are the Lord God of Israel.'

The wet wood and the body of the bull suddenly burst into flames and clouds of hissing steam and smoke swirled into the air. The people fell on their faces and praised God.

The priests of Baal were driven down the mountain and were killed by the people. Then Elijah went back to the top of Mount Carmel and looked out to the west where the blue Mediterranean Sea glinted in the late afternoon sun. Rising from the sea he saw a small cloud. 'King Ahab,' said the prophet, 'ride quickly back in your chariot. I smell rain. The drought will soon be over as the Lord God wishes.'

Ahab galloped in his chariot and Elijah ran ahead; and the sky grew dark. Soon great spots of rain began to fall and very soon it was pouring down in torrents on the dry and dusty earth.

*

Naboth's vineyard

Next to the royal palace of King Ahab of Israel there lived a man called Naboth. Naboth owned a small piece of land by the palace wall where he grew grapes, as had his father and his fathers before him.

One day King Ahab sent for Naboth. 'I would like to buy your vineyard, Naboth. I want to make myself a bigger vegetable garden and your vineyard would do very nicely. You can either have money for it, or I can give you a much better vineyard than the one you have now.'

'I'm sorry, your Majesty,' replied Naboth nervously, 'but my father and his fathers have owned this land for many many years, and I cannot sell it.'

King Ahab sulked angrily and refused to eat his supper that night. Queen Jezebel spoke gently to him to find out the reason for his bad temper, and he told her: 'And there is nothing I can do about it. I must obey the law like everyone else.'

But Queen Jezebel was a princess of Phoenicia where kings and princes did whatever they liked: 'A fine king of Israel you make! If you want Naboth's vineyard, I shall get it for you.'

Jezebel went off and wrote some letters, signing them in King Ahab's own name.

She wrote to the mayor and council of the town telling them that Naboth had been swearing against God and threatening to fight against the King. Two witnesses must be found, Naboth must be found guilty and stoned to death.

The mayor and his friends weren't such brave people as Naboth. They did not dare stand up to the King. Everyone knew that Naboth had done nothing wrong, and yet two men were found to say they had heard Naboth swearing against God and threatening to fight against the King. The mayor and his council found Naboth guilty of treason for which the punishment was death by stoning. So the innocent Naboth died because of the trickery and lies of the wicked Queen Jezebel.

When Jezebel heard that Naboth was dead, she came to the King. 'Husband, Naboth, whose vineyard you want so much, has been found guilty of plotting to kill you. He has been executed. You must know that any land belonging to a man executed for treason belongs to his King. Go and take Naboth's vineyard.'

King Ahab was delighted. Immediately he gave orders for the palace wall to be knocked down and rebuilt around Naboth's vineyard so that he could have a bigger vegetable patch.

When the prophet Elijah heard the story of Naboth's vineyard, he was extremely angry. Quite unafraid Elijah came to Ahab. 'I have found you out. I have found out your trickery. I have found out how Naboth was murdered. You know you have done wrong in the sight of God and both you and the Queen your wife will come to disaster.

Elijah's words meant nothing to the wicked Jezebel, but Ahab was truly sorry for what had happened. He tore off his fine royal clothes and dressed in sackcloth. He fasted and walked everywhere slowly and miserable, and Elijah knew that he was sorry for his wicked deeds.

Three years later Ahab did come to a disastrous end, although he faced it with courage. In a battle against the King of Syria, Ahab was hit in the chest by a stray arrow. Ahab knew that he was dying and that the battle would be lost if his soldiers knew it. He had himself propped up in his chariot facing the enemy to encourage his men. There throughout the day as the fighting raged Ahab slowly bled to death, dying with the setting of the sun.

It was twelve years after this that Queen Jezebel faced her disaster. Ahab's son was now king but one of his own captains shot him with an arrow and seized the royal palace. Hearing the news Jezebel went up to her room, combed her hair and put on her make-up, and was then flung out of the window by the captain's men.

As for Elijah, he had died some years before. A group of holy men had come to see Elijah, and as they were talking, a chariot and horses of fire came down from heaven. Elijah stepped onto the chariot and was whisked away in a whirlwind never to be seen again.

*

Elijah stood on Mount Sinai and God himself came by. There was a great wind so strong that it tore the mountains and shattered the rocks as God came by. But the Lord was not in the wind. After the wind there was an earthquake. But the Lord was not in the earthquake. After the earthquake there came fire. But the Lord was not in the fire. And after the fire there came a still small voice like a gentle breeze. When Elijah heard it he covered his face with his cloak and stood at the mouth of his cave. 'Why are you here, Elijah?', said a voice. 'Because I am faithful to the Lord God of All Peoples,' answered the prophet.

(*from* 1 Kings 19:11-14)

*

The Prophet Jeremiah

The story and sayings of the prophet Jeremiah can be found in the Books of Jeremiah, Baruch *and* Lamentations *where the attempts of the prophet to keep the Jewish people to their covenant with God can be seen against the background of the great movements of power between the Assyrian, Babylonian and Egyptian empires with the tiny state of Judah caught between. He bitterly denounced the slide away from monotheism and the influence of foreign religious cults which involved worship of various gods, witchcraft and even child-sacrifice. But he held out the hope of God as a father and friend who would forgive the sincerely repentant.*

Jeremiah was born about 650 BCE in a small village a few kilometres north of Jerusalem of a priestly family and began his ministry at about the age of twenty. During his lifetime the Babylonian Empire ascended over the Assyrian; its king, Nebuchadrezzar II, (ruled 605-562 BCE) sacking Jerusalem and exiling its leading inhabitants (perhaps 40 000 of them) to Babylon. The remnant of Jews were governed by Gedaliah who had been appointed by the Babylonian king. The significance of his assassination is that the reprisals ended all chances of Jewish autonomy. Jeremiah died in Egypt. It is not known when.

Some Jews hold the Fast of Gedaliah on the 3rd of the month of Tishri which falls in September to commemorate the scattering of the Jews.

*

Jeremiah and the scattering of the Jews

The old prophet Jeremiah was not much liked in Jerusalem. He spoke the words God told him and the people did not want to hear them. He had seen kings come and go and had told them all the same thing: that they and their people must worship the one God as Moses had shown them in the days of old. But no-one wanted to listen and everyone laughed when he said that Jerusalem and its Temple would be destroyed as a punishment.

But Jeremiah was right. King Nebuchadrezzar of Babylon destroyed the city of Jerusalem. The city walls were torn down, every house was damaged, the palace of the king lay smouldering and the great Temple of Solomon could hardly be recognized. There were very few people left in the city: only the very poor and some Jewish freedom-fighters who had managed to escape. The king, the priests, the soldiers, the shopkeepers, the rich and the clever, in fact all the people a city needs to keep it going, had all been taken as prisoners to the city of Babylon where Nebuchadrezzar had his capital.

Jeremiah's life was spared and he was allowed to live in the village where the new governor was. Governor Gedaliah sent out a message to all the Jews left in the land. He called to him all the fighting bands from out of their hiding places and they came to a meeting at the governor's house.

'There is nothing to fear,' announced Gedaliah. 'Orders have come from King Nebuchadrezzar himself that you may live peacefully in the land of Judah as long as you pay your tax and do nothing against the Babylonian king.'

This was exactly what Jeremiah had been saying for years. And no-one had taken any notice of him.

'Most of our people have been taken as prisoners to Babylon,' said Johanon who was one of the rebel leaders, 'but this means that the few of us who are left can begin to make a nation of Jews again.'

The news spread to the countries round about and the Jews who had escaped as refugees began to come back to settle down and work their farms once more. After the greatest disaster that anyone could imagine, Jerusalem destroyed and the Temple knocked down, it seemed that the Jewish people might still have a chance to live as a nation in peace.

However, it came to Johanon's ears that a band of freedom-fighters led by Ishmael ben Nethaniah had been paid by a foreign king to murder Gedaliah. Johanon went to see the governor.

'I don't believe it,' replied Gedaliah. 'Ishmael is one of the Jewish freedom-fighters. His men fought well against Nebuchadrezzar's Babylonian army. I'm sorry, Johanon, but I can't take it seriously.'

'Look, let me take my men and secretly kill Ishmael before he kills you,' said Johanon. 'I'm not just thinking of you. Without you as our governor the Jewish people will all be lost.'

'No, Johanon,' replied Gedaliah. 'I know that you mean well but your information about Ishmael must be wrong.'

And, to show that he had nothing to worry about, Gedaliah invited Ishmael and his band of men to a meal at the governor's house. Ishmael and ten of his men sat down to a friendly meal with Gedaliah. And when the food was eaten and the wine had been drunk Ishmael's men murdered Gedaliah and everyone in the house.

The next day they killed seventy pilgrims on their way to visit the ruined Temple and rounded up all the people left in the town as hostages. Then they set out for the land of the foreign king to claim their money.

It was not long before Johanon heard what had happened and he gathered his men and set off with the other leaders in search of Ishmael.

They caught up with him at the town of Gibeon where they attacked his gang by the side of a great pool. It was a short affair. The people Ishmael was holding as hostages all escaped to Johanon's side and Ishmael and most of his men escaped to the foreign king's country.

Ishmael had been driven from the land, but the problems were not all solved. Johanon was afraid that the Babylonian soldiers would take revenge on all the Jews for the murder of Gedaliah. There was a great deal of discussion and argument as to what to do. Most people voted to go to Egypt. It had been peaceful there for some time now and there was said to be food in plenty. Johanon decided that Jeremiah must be asked. After all he had been quite right about Nebuchadrezzar destroying Jerusalem and so his word was now held in great respect.

'As you can see,' said Johanon to the prophet Jeremiah, 'there are only a few of us left out of a whole nation. We ask you for the word of God on what we should do.'

'I shall pray to God as you ask,' answered Jeremiah, 'and I shall tell you exactly what He tells me, whether I think you will like it or not.'

'We will do whatever you tell us we must do, whether we like it or not. We will obey the Lord our God.'

Ten days later Jeremiah sent for the leaders of the people. The prophet told them not to run away to Egypt as refugees but to stay in their own land of Judah. If they stayed the Babylonians would do them no harm, but if they went to Egypt there would be war and famine.

'No,' cried Johanon, 'you're not telling us the truth. How can we be safe here when the Babylonians suspect us of killing their governor? We will all be killed if we stay here in Judah. The best thing we can do is to go to Egypt. When things have quietened down here we can come back.'

'If you leave Judah for Egypt,' replied the prophet, 'not one of you will ever return. I'm only telling you what God has told me: if you go to Egypt every one of you will die there of disease or hunger or war.'

Like many people before him Johanon had asked for God's word from Jeremiah and promised to do whatever God said. Now Johanon changed his mind. Jews from throughout the land came to join the refugees and, led by Johanon, they set off towards Egypt taking Jeremiah with them.

And in Egypt Jeremiah died. In Egypt, too, died every man and woman and child who had fled from Judah. As Jeremiah had told them, not one returned.

*

Much of what Jeremiah said had to do with war and death and the anger of God against a wicked people who had forgotten Him. But Jeremiah was a prophet with a message of hope — hope that the people of Judah would one day return to their country and hope that the people would come back to God and live their lives as He wants them to.

These are the words of the Lord:
Shout with joy for Israel's sake,
lead the nations, crying loud and clear,
singing out your praises and saying:
The Lord has saved his people,
those that are left of Israel.
Look, I will bring them back from the land of the north
and I will gather them from the far ends of the earth;
all of them: the blind and the lame,
women with child and women in labour,
a great company of people.
They will come home in tears,
but I will comfort them as I lead them back.
I will lead them to flowing streams
by a smooth path so they shall not stumble,
for I am a father to Israel.

(*from* The Book of Jeremiah 31:7-9)

*

This is the contract I will make with the people of Israel in days to come, said the Lord. I will set my law deep within them and write it on their hearts. Then I will be their God and they shall be my people. They will no longer need to teach each other to know the Lord. They will all know me, the highest and the lowest, said the Lord, for I will forgive the wrong things they have done and I will remember their sins no more.

(*from* The Book of Jeremiah 31:33-34)

Rabbi Akiba

*Jewish tradition recognizes the religious authority of both the Written and the Oral
Law, the former being found in the Five Books attributed to the prophet Moses
(c.14th century BCE), Genesis, Exodus, Leviticus, Numbers, and Deuteronomy col-
lectively known as the Torah (the Law) and held to be the revelation by God of
Himself to man. The Oral Law is collected from many authorities in the Talmud
and is the interpretation of the Law to suit the particular needs of the age. Rabbi
Akiba was certainly the greatest of the voluntary profession of rabbis who followed
the pharasaic tradition in continuing the development of the Oral Law and was
a central figure in Judaism at a time when its people and religion might well have
disappeared with little trace.*

*Akiba was born about 40 CE into a landless peasant family near the coastal town
of Lydda in Palestine during the insensitive and often cruel Roman occupation.
In 70 CE after nationalist insurrections in Judea, Jerusalem was captured and the
Temple destroyed so completely that only the Western Wall remains. A further revolt
was mercilessly suppressed in 115 CE and in 132 CE Simeon Bar Kokhba's rebellion
and its disastrous aftermath led to the destruction of Judea. Akiba had learned
to read at the age of 40 and was accepted as the foremost authority on the interpretation of the law. Unable to compromise with the Roman law of 132 CE forbidding study of the Torah he was cruelly executed at the age of 97.*

*

Akiba learns to read

Nearly two thousand years ago there lived in Palestine a shepherd boy called Akiba.
All Akiba's family worked for a rich farmer, but they were desperately poor. The
farmer lived in a great house surrounded by beautiful gardens with all sorts of
food in plenty and servants and slaves to do whatever he wished. But Akiba lived
in a small square hut made of mudbrick: it had a low door, but no windows, no
furniture and nothing to cover the bare earth floor but straw.

As he sat guarding his master's sheep Akiba would usually feel hungry. His
family always ate the same things: every day, with any luck, there would be heavy
rough bread, and sometimes there was raw cabbage or turnip. Cooked food was
really only for rich people who could afford burn fires to boil water.

Times were hard for most people in Palestine. The country was ruled by the
Romans. Akiba never saw much of the Roman soldiers but they were well known
for their bullying and cruelty.

Everything wasn't bad for Akiba. He lived an outdoor life in a warm country which was green with growing plants. Behind him the hills of Judea shimmered in the heat haze; in front was the clear blue sky and the shining blue of the Mediterranean Sea. It was hot and sunny in summer and warm and sunny in winter with cool refreshing rain.

And so Akiba grew up into a tall strong man. He could not read or write and didn't want to learn. The only people he had ever come across who could read were rich conceited people: they didn't think much of a poor boy, and Akiba didn't think much of them.

But things were soon to change. Akiba met a woman from a better family than his called Rachel. Her father wouldn't even let Akiba into his house — he would have nothing to do with a poor and ignorant shepherd. And Rachel herself believed that Akiba could do better for himself. So when he asked her to marry him she said no, not unless he learned to read and write. He agreed and the two were married.

Akiba found a rabbi, a priest who was willing to teach him to read, and he began to study. After a long day out under a hot sun looking after the sheep Akiba would plod wearily home only to have to struggle all evening with his letters. Every day until it grew dark he would go through his alphabet trying to remember the names and sound of each letter. And when he had begun to get the hang of most of them the rabbi gave him a book to read. It was not one of the famous Jewish stories such as Noah and the Ark, or Adam and Eve, or Moses or Joseph and his many-coloured coat. Akiba was expected to read the Book of Leviticus which gives technical details of the sacrificial offerings and complicated rules of behaviour which even a priest might have difficulty with. Akiba really couldn't manage it — after a hard day's work to have to read such things was too much for him, and he gave up.

But his wife Rachel did not give up. She was determined that Akiba should succeed. One day while he tended the sheep Akiba came to a spring of water. The water gushed out of a hole in the hill and fell as a small waterfall on to a rock beneath. And where the water hit the rock, day after day, year after year, it had worn away a groove. He realised that his wife was right. Just as the water had worn away the hard rock by pouring on to it, he too must keep on trying and trying until he had learned to read.

He came home and took his five year old son with him to the rabbi. 'Teach us both,' he asked the rabbi, 'and we will learn to read together.'

And so Akiba began again. By helping his son to learn to read it made it easier for him. Father and son did learn together. It was not long before Akiba overtook his son and he studied the Book of Moses, the writings of the Prophets and the other books of the Bible. It had taken him until he was 40 years old, but he had learned to read. He decided to become a rabbi himself so that he could teach others, not only to read, but to understand the word of God as he had come to understand it in the Bible.

Akiba went to the rabbis' academy which was like a university for priests and a place where the law of the Bible was discussed and decided upon. First he went to Eliezeryben Hyrkanos, one of the men who had begun the academy. Eliezer might well be the one to teach him. He had been brought up as a peasant and knew what it was like to be poor and hungry. He was rich and famous now but surely he would remember. Indeed he did remember and that was the reason he turned Akiba away. 'I won't be able to teach you anything,' said Eliezer. 'You'll be so busy worrying about not having enough food for your family that you won't be able to concentrate. Come back when you're richer.'

But one of the other teachers there offered to help. He too had been poor and had taught himself the Bible while he nearly starved. He taught Akiba himself and sent him to other wise rabbis. Akiba studied for thirteen years before he felt that he could come back to the rabbis' academy to discuss the Bible and the law with Eliezer and the other teachers there. After spending some time listening to what was said Akiba came to the point where he could not agree. And so he stood up, a newcomer to the academy, and argued with Eliezer himself. And he argued so clearly and so well, he knew and understood the Bible so perfectly that Eliezer had to admit that he was right.

As time went by it became clear to everyone at the academy that Akiba was cleverer than them all. He was appointed to the committee in charge and was so important to the rabbis there that when he went away for a time, one of them said, it seemed as if the Bible had gone.

*

Jews believe that learning is very important, and that reading and understanding and being able to interpret what the Bible says are most important of all. This prayer is one of the Blessings read daily in synagogue services:

> You favour men with knowledge
> and teach us understanding.
> May You continue to favour us
> with knowledge and understanding and learning
> for all these things come from You.
> We praise You, O Lord,
> gracious Giver of knowledge.

(*from the* Fourth Blessing of the Tefillah)

Akiba's death

Rabbi Akiba was a man of great importance, known by learned scholars of the Bible and loved by the ordinary people too. He had struggled to learn to read when he was middle-aged and had taught himself so much about the Bible that he had become a rabbi and joined the rabbis academy. But he never forgot that he had once been a poor shepherd — when he was asked to join the committee that was in charge of the academy he took as his special job the care of the poor people.

When he opened a school for students who wanted to study the Bible with him, he treated them as if they were his own children. One student became ill and had no-one to look after him. Rabbi Akiba acted as nurse and looked after him and cooked and cleaned until he was better.

Although he was a famous man he still believed it was important to carry on teaching the young. He had found that learning to read had been extremely difficult, but reading had given him everying that had made him famous — knowledge, understanding and wisdom.

He described a teacher and his students like this: a lemon tree gives off a sweet smell which people enjoy, a candle can light another candle giving us twice the amount of light, a stream gives refreshing water for us to drink. Although the tree and the candle and stream have all given something, they have lost nothing. And so it is with a teacher who gives his skills to his students.

Palestine 2000 years ago was occupied by the Romans. When Akiba was a young man there had been a rebellion and the Jews had tried to beat the Romans. The Jews were crushed and the Romans had destroyed the city of Jerusalem and burned the Temple. Thousands of Jews had been sold as slaves or executed. Things had quietened down since then. Probably the Jews had lost the will to fight against such a cruel enemy. And as things became more peaceful the Romans treated the Jews more kindly.

Now Akiba was an old man. He lived in hope, like every other Jew, that one day the great Temple would be built again in Jerusalem, but there seemed very little chance of that. However, Hadrian who was now the emperor had been studying reports from that part of the Empire. It seemed silly to him to have destroyed Jerusalem when there were no other great cities in that part of the world. The Roman Empire needed cities for cities were places where money was to be made. And so Emperor Hadrian informed the Jews that Jerusalem could be rebuilt and so could the Temple.

That was the good news. the bad news was that Emperor Hadrian wanted the Temple to have a statue of him dressed up as Jupiter, king of the Roman gods. The Jews worship one God who cannot be shown as a statue because He is a spirit. There could be nothing worse than to have God's sacred Temple dedicated to a Roman emperor dressed up as a god.

Rabbi Akiba who was now 90 years old was bitterly disappointed as were the rest of the Jewish nation. Before trouble could begin the Roman solderies arrested Rabbi Ishmael and Rabbi Simeon, two men who would have been very likely to lead a revolt. They bravely went to their deaths praying for their people.

Akiba spoke over their graves and warned the Jews: 'Perpare to suffer,' he said. 'God has taken away the best of us so that they shall not suffer.'

Akiba was right though it did not seem so at first. A Jewish soldier called Simeon bar Kokhba started to gather young men to him to fight against the Romans. And to the Jews' surprise and joy they managed to beat a well-armed well-trained Roman army. But not for long. The Romans turned their anger on Judea and within three years the land had been emptied of people – thousands were sold as slaves, thousands fled to other countries and hundreds of thousands were killed. The few Jews that remained were forbidden to practise their religion or to teach the Jewish way of life to their children.

Akiba had been allowed to live, perhaps because he was so old they thought he could cause no trouble. But the fury of the Romans was not over. a law was passed now forbidding rabbis to teach the Bible or even to study it. Akiba realised that the Jewish religion could survive without the Temple, without Jerusalem, even without the rabbis, but if Jews were not allowed to read and study the Bible their religion would surely die.

Akiba openly called his students to him and they read and discussed the Bible. It did not take long for the Roman soldiers to arrive. He was arrested and put into prison.

But the Romans were quite kind to the old rabbi. He was allowed to have his old students and friends visit him. And when they did Akiba taught them about the Bible. He was moved to a far-away prison and soon brought to trial. The sentence was death.

Akiba, 97 years old, was led out to his execution at dawn He was to be killed by having the flesh torn from his body. Wounded and bleeding and in terrible pain he watched as the sun rose above the horizon and he began to sing the Jewish morning prayer from the Bible:

'Hear, O Israel:
the Lord is our God,
the Lord is One.

We praise his name
whose glorious kingdom is for ever and ever.

And you shall love the Lord your God
with all your heart,
and with all your soul,
and with all your might.'

The Roman general was amazed that he could speak so clearly and calmly while suffering so much pain. He asked, 'Are you a wizard or do you feel no pain?'

'Neither,' replied Akiba. 'I have always loved God with all my heart and soul and might. Now I know that I love Him with all my life too.'

Akiba began again: 'Hear, O Israel: the Lord is our God, the Lord is One.' And with these words he died.

*

Tobit

The Book of Tobit does not appear in the Hebrew canon but can be found in the Septuagint, the verion of the Bible traditionally translated by 70 scholars into Greek in Alexandria during the 2nd century BCE. It was the most commonly used version among Jews of the Dispersion whose mother-tongue was usually Greek, the lingua franca of that time. (Tobit and other additional books of the Septuagint are accepted as canon by Roman Catholic and Orthodox Christians, and as Apocrypha by Protestant Christians.)

Tobit was possibly written as early as the 4th century BCE and possibly in Hebrew, though the story is set some time after the fall of the northern kingdom of Israel in 722 BCE (so Shalmanezer V could not have been Tobit's master: he died in 722.) Assyria was ruled from Nineveh (near modern Mosul in northern Iraq); the capital of Media was Ecbatana some 600 km to the west (modern Hamadan in Iran). Raphael is one of the seven archangels of God (Gabriel and Michael are named in the Bible; the others are traditionally Jeremiel, Raguel, Sariel and Uriel). Asmodeus is the King of the Demons — his name means 'the Destroyer'. The story of Tobit is a stand against foreign cultural and religious influences on Judaism and represents a call to return to the traditions of the Mosaic law with its dependence on one universal God with whom the Jewish people felt they had a special relationship.

*

Blind Tobit

Tobit couldn't work because he was blind. The family had to live on the small amount of money earned by Tobit's wife, Anna who was a weaver.

But things had not always been like this. Even though Tobit was a foreigner, a Jew living in Nineveh, he had once been the buyer of supplies for the Emperor of Assyria, King Shalmanezer. Tobit travelled around Assyria buying things the King needed and he also went to other countries and soon became very rich. Tobit had made so much money that he had left ten full bags of silver for safe-keeping with a cousin of his in the land of Media. Unfortunately the roads had become unsafe to travel and he was never able to get the money back.

Tobit had been rich but he was never mean. Lots of Jews lived in Nineveh, but most of them were poor and many of them were slaves. Tobit gave food to the hungry and clothes to the poor. When the soldiers killed Jews and left their bodies to rot in the street Tobit would himself go out and bury them properly. But now Tobit was blind and poor.

One day Anna sold some cloth. Not only was she paid for it but given a young goat as well. Tobit heard the goat bleating. 'Where have you got that goat from, Anna?' asked Tobit. 'I know you have stolen it, because we haven't enough money to buy a goat.'

When Anna told him the truth, Tobit was deeply ashamed. In despair he prayed that God would let him die.

As Tobit said his prayer, four hundred miles away in the land of Media a distant relation of Tobit's was also at prayer. Sarah lived at Ecbatana, the capital city of Media and she was tormented by the King of the Demons, Asmodeus, the Destroyer. Although she was still young, Sarah had lost seven husbands. Each time her father had found her someone to marry, the devil Asmodeus had killed him before the wedding night. In despair Sarah prayed that God would let her die.

God heard their prayers at the same time and he sent the angel Raphael to help these two good people.

Back in Nineveh Tobit was making arrangements in case he should die. He called his son Tobias to him. 'Tobias,' said Tobit, 'if I should die, I want you to make sure that I am properly buried. Look after your mother, Anna and find yourself a good wife from our people. Give to the poor and never do anything to other people that you would hate them to do to you. Always praise God and pray to him for help.'

'I will, Father,' replied Tobias.

'And now I have a job for you. Some years ago I left ten bags of silver with my cousin in Media. I know the roads are dangerous, but if you are brave enough, and you can find someone to show you the way, you can go and collect the money.'

Tobias went to ask if anyone knew the way across the mountains to Media and he came upon a young man called Raphael. Raphael said he would be glad to help.

Tobias and Raphael travelled until night fell and then camped by the side of the River Tigris. As Tobias bathed his aching feet a large fish grabbed hold of his toe. 'Don't let it go!' shouted Raphael. Tobias held tight as the fish wriggled and managed to get it to land. That night as they ate the fish Raphael told Tobias to save the heart and liver of the fish because they could be used as medicine.

Apart from the hardships of travelling on foot over the mountain roads Tobias and Raphael met no dangers and after many days travel they came to Ecbatana in the land of Media. Tobias was surprised how much Raphael seemed to know about his family. He told Tobias that the boy had a distant relation in Ecbatana, a young woman called Sarah. They could stay at her house for a time.

Sarah's father and mother were delighted to see their relation from Nineveh. During the evening meal the father told Tobias the sad story of Sarah's seven husbands and of the wicked demon Asmodeus. Raphael spoke quietly to Tobias, 'This is the girl you should marry. She is one of your own people.'

'But what about this devil who has killed seven young men so far?' asked Tobias trembling.

'Do you still have the fish's heart? On your wedding night, when Asmodeus appears, throw the heart on to a burning candle. This is sure to drive the demon away.'

Neither Sarah nor her parents knew whether to be pleased or sad when Tobias asked if he could marry Sarah. They were glad that he wanted to marry their daughter, but they were unhappy at the thought of losing yet another son-in-law. But Raphael promised that all would be well. The wedding took place that same day.

That night before Tobias and Sarah went to bed, they prayed that God would protect them. Tobias made sure that a candle was burning and that he had the fish's heart ready. The very moment that Asmodeus made his appearance Tobias quickly threw the fish heart on to the candle flame. The cloud of choking black smoke smelt terrible. And it clearly smelt terrible to the demon as well, for as soon as it reached his nostrils he turned and fled. That night, as Tobias and Sarah slept peacefully, Raphael chased Asmodeus across land and sea to Egypt where he tied him hand and foot.

In the morning Sarah's parents were full of joy to find Tobias still alive. Her father had even dug a grave for him that night, certain that the demon would kill him. They praised God and a feast was prepared to celebrate the marriage.

However, Tobias was worried that his father would be concerned that the journey was taking such a long time and asked Raphael if he would visit his father's cousin to collect the ten bags of silver. Raphael did this and the ten bags were handed over to him.

And so, after the wedding celebrations were over, there were many tears and much laughter as Tobias and his wife Sarah followed Raphael on the long journey back to Nineveh.

Anna had been waiting anxiously in Nineveh as had Tobit. Each day she would stand and gaze down the road that led to Ecbatana looking for Tobias, and each day she would come home to tell Tobit that there was no sign of him. At night she would weep and cry and not be able to sleep. But one day she saw three people coming along the road, and one of them she recognised immediately as her son. As she ran to him and flung her arms around his neck, she called out to Tobit that their son had returned. Poor Tobit blindly stumbled out through the doorway to meet Tobias.

'Do you still have the fish liver that I told you to keep,' said Raphael to Tobias. Tobias said he had. 'You remember I told you that it was medicine. If you rub it on your father's eyes, you will give him back his sight.'

And so it was done. As Tobias rubbed Tobit's eyes with the fish's liver, Tobit began to see, in a blur at first, but soon quite clearly. 'Praise be to God!' shouted Tobit, full of excitement. 'I can see my son, Tobias.'

When Tobit and Anna met their daughter-in-law, Sarah, there was great rejoicing and all the Jews of Nineveh shared the family's happiness.

After the second wedding feast was over, Tobit and Tobias spoke to Raphael to offer him five of the ten bags of silver. after all it had been Raphael who had arranged the marriage and Raphael who had given Tobit back his sight.

Raphael spoke to them in a serious voice: 'I am Raphael, one of God's angels. I have done nothing for you, but thank God for what he has done. Live a life as you have done, giving food to the hungry, clothes and money to the poor, and tell everyone how good God has been to you.'

With these words Raphael rose. Tobias and Tobit knelt down before him, and when they looked again he was gone. Tobit and Tobias did as Raphael had said and they were long remembered for their good deeds by the Jews of Nineveh and Ecbatana.

*

Happy are the people who love God!
Happy are the people who rejoice in God's peace!
Happy are the people who are sorry that they have
   been punished by God!
For they will soon rejoice in God
   and share His joy for ever.
My soul praises the Lord, the great King,
   for His kingdom will last for ever and ever.

(*from* Tobit 13:14-19)

*

Judith

The Book of Judith stands in the same category as that of Tobit (qv.) It is not accepted in the Hebrew canon but can be found in the Septuagint, the Greek version of the Bible which held a dominant position amongst the Greek-speaking Jews of the Dispersion. It is also the accepted version of the Old Testament used by most Christians throughout the world.

Judith seems to have been written sometime during the 2nd century BCE when Israel was struggling against the enforced hellenisation of the Seleucid Empire. The action of the story, however, is much earlier, set during the time of King Nebuchadnezzar of Babylon. According to the story, Nebuchadnezzar's army was repulsed; in fact, they sacked Jerusalem in 587 BCE and large numbers of Jews were deported to Babylon. Most modern interpreters would hold that, although not factually true, the story is valid scripture in that it contains more profound truths than historical ones.

*

Judith and Holofernes

The anger of King Nebuchadnezzar was great and his memory was long. Nebuchadnezzar never forgot the day when he was fighting the armies of the Assyrian Emperor, when he had asked the countries round about for their help. They hadn't even sent him an answer. But Nebuchadnezzar had beaten the Assyrians and was now the King of Babylon, the greatest empire the world had ever known.

Nebuchadnezzar called Holofernes, his best general before him. 'General Holofernes, these are your orders from the Great King of the Whole World. Take a hundred and thirty thousand of my finest roops and punish all those countries that refused to help me when I asked them to. Smother the land with my army and let my soldiers steal whatever they want. The dead will fill the valleys and every stream and river will be choked with bodies. Do not disobey my orders, Holofernes, and carry them out straight away.

General Holofernes did as his king ordered and swept throught the nearby countries with his thousands of men and followers. Fields were burned, villages, towns and cities were knocked down and the people killed were too many to count.

At last Holofernes came to the land of the Israelites. He knew that they had set soldiers to guard the mountain roads into the country and he was determined to teach them a lesson. But he needed information about his enemy, how strong they were, how big was their army, who was their leader, and so on. So Holofernes sent for the leaders of the neighbouring countries and asked them.

Achoir, the leader of the Ammonites dared to speak: he told Holofernes the history of the Isralelites, how they believed in one God who protected them when they were faithful to him and punished them when they forgot him. 'So my lord Holofernes, if the Israelites have been wicked and forgotten their God, you will be able to beat them easily; but if they have been faithful to their God there is no power on earth that can defeat them.'

Holofernes flew into a rage when he heard this. 'I can beat anyone with my army,' he shouted. 'I shall wipe them out. The mountains will be drenched with their blood and the fields will be full of their dead bodies. And if you think that they are so strong, you had better go and join them.

And so Achior was sent over to the Israelites in the nearby town of Bethulia where he was welcomed warmly.

By now Holofernes had an army of over 180 000 soldiers. Marching orders were given and they all set out to attack the small mountain town of Bethulia. After that Holofernes planned to sweep across the land burning and killing until he reached Jerusalem. But Bethulia was not going to be easy to capture. It stood high on a hill and had strong walls. 'General,' said one of the soldiers, 'you don't need to attack the town. If you surround Bethulia with our army and stop the Israelites getting to the wells and rivers for water, they will soon have to give up and we won't lose any men fighting.'

Thirty four days later things in Bethulia were getting desperate. There was hardly any water left in the town and people were fainting in the streets. If anyone had the strength to climb the city wall they could look down and see the great army surrounding the town. In the hot summer sunshine the enemy soldiers gambled or joked or practised with their swords, and they all had food and water in plenty.

The Israelites gathered in the town square and begged the mayor to surrender. 'It would be better to be captured by Holofernes' army than to die of thirst,' they shouted.

Now there lived in Bethulia a rich widow called Judith. Her husband had died three years before and, although she was young and beautiful, she always wore the black clothes of a widow. When Judith heard that the people wanted to surrender, she was ashamed of their lack of faith in God. Judith went to the mayor. 'Don't you trust God any more. You cannot give up. God will do with us what he thinks best.'

The mayor was ashamed that he had thought of surrendering and agreed with Judith. 'I have a plan,' said Judith, 'and I believe God will help me in it.'

'May God go with you,' said the mayor.

Judith went back home and prayed for God's help. Then she took off her black widow's dress and put on her brightest clothes; she did her hair and put on her best jewellery: rings, bracelets, anklets, earrings and necklaces. After she had put on her most expensive perfume, Judith packed a small bag of food and set out for the city gate. The people there hardly recognised her and they all stared in amazement as she went out of the gate and began walking towards the enemy camp.

As soon as Judith crossed into enemy territory she was seized by Holofernes' soldiers who first questioned her and then took her to the General himself.

Holofernes was pleased to see such a beautiful woman coming over to his side. 'No harm will come to you, madam,' he said, 'and you will be well treated in my camp.'

'General, I have come here to tell you how you can defeat the Israelites,' said Judith, praying that God would forgive her for telling lies to Holofernes. 'You know that our God will protect us while we do not forget him. But now the people of Bethulia are so hungry that they are going to eat the harvest food given to God in the Temple. When they do this God will punish them by letting your army defeat the Israelites.'

'But how will I know when the Israelites have eaten this holy food?'

'I shall stay with you and go out each night to pray,' said Judith. 'I will tell you when the time is right.'

For three days Judith stayed in the enemy camp and each day Holofernes was attracted to her more and more. On the fourth day the General held a banquet for Judith. She dressed in her finest clothes and Holofernes offered the best in food and drink. Judith would touch none of it and ate the food she had brought with her. Holofernes drank the wine and ate and drank some more and at length sent his servants away so that he could be alone with Judith.

By now the General's head was beginning to spin. He had drunk too much and he started to feel sleepy. Holofernes lay on his bed and was soon fast in a drunken sleep. Judith prayed to God to give her strength. Then she took Holofernes' own great war-sword in one hand, and holding his hair in the other, she struck twice at the General's neck and cut off his head. Quickly she emptied her food bag and put the head into it. Calmly she walked out of the tent and into the darkness as if she was going to say her evening prayers. The guards did not know, of course, that when she disappeared into the night, she did not stop to pray but kept on walking back to Bethulia.

'Open the gates!' shouted Judith and guards came rushing. When it was known what Judith had done and what it was she carried in her bag, the people of the town got out of their beds and thanked God.

'Hang the head of Holofernes from the city wall,' said Judith, 'and get all our men armed and ready. When the sun rises we will attack the enemy!'

As the dawn broke Holofernes' guards suddenly saw the Israelites standing with their weapons outside the city walls as if ready to attack. They were astounded at the sight for they knew that after a month and a half there was not food and very little water in Bethulia and that the people were weak and ill. Besides, they all expected the victory that Judith had promised.

Messengers were sent to wake up General Holofernes. His servant called but there was no reply. When Holofernes headless body was found sprawled inside the tent and there was no sign of Judith, it was clear what had happened.

The news spread throughout Holofernes' army and the soldiers in fear and dismay began to pack their things and run. Within hours the campsite had been deserted and the great army was being chased from Israel.

In Bethulia there was singing and dancing after the dangers they had all been through. Then Judith and many of the people went up to the Temple in Jerusalem and gave their thanks to God.

*

Lord, you are great and glorious;
your stength is wonderful, no-one could defeat you.
Let all living things serve you!
For when you spoke everything was created,
and when you breathed everything was made.
No-one can stand against you.
If the mountains fell into the sea
and the rocks melted like wax,
you would still show mercy
to people who worship you.
To offer you sweetly smelling incense is a very little thing
and all the sacrifices in the world are not enough,
but anyone who fears the Lord will be great forever.

(from The Book of Judith 16:13-17)

*

The Maccabees

The Revolt of the Maccabees, beginning in 167 BCE, is told in the Book of Maccabees to be found in the Septuagint. It was a remarkable stand for the preservation of Jewish religious, cultural and political identity in the face of the hellenising policies of the Seleucid Empire, in particular King Antiochus IV of Syria (born c.215 BCE, ruled c.175-163) who wanted to restore the Empire to the former glories of Alexander the Great's reign. The village priest from Modin near Lydda, Mattathias passed the leadership of the revolt to Judah the Maccabee ('the Hammer') (leader 166-161 BCE); his youngest brother, Jonathan led until his treacherous murder in 142 BCE and was followed by the second youngest brother, Simon who was also betrayed and murdered by his son-in-law. John the eldest of the brothers was ambushed and killed and the story of the death of Eleazar in 162 BCE is retold here. The dynasty later named Hasmonean after an ancestor of Mattathias, lasted until Herod the Great was made king by Caesar Augustus in 37 BCE.

*

The bravery of Eleazar the Maccabee

Mattathias the Maccabee was an old Jewish priest. He was ordered by the Greek soldiers of King Antiochus of Syria to make sacrifices to the Greek gods, but he refused. In a fit of anger he seized the sword of the Greek officer and killed him. Mattathias and his five sons escaped into the desert.

But Mattathias was an old man and the strain of fighting the King's men became too much for him. As he was dying he said 'Never forget the great things that our people have done in the past. They have stayed true to God and He has helped them. Wicked people may seem to do well, but everything they do will end in dust and ashes.'

It took his son, Judah two and a half years of struggle to win back the right to worship the true God. Many a battle was fought and many lives were lost before Judah was able to cleanse the Temple and hold the great service of rejoicing, still remembered to this day.

But the Greek King of Syria did not forget or forgive the victory won by the Maccabees.

General Lysais was angry. His trained Greek soldiers had been beaten by Jewish peasants led by the Maccabee brothers, and he was determined to wipe them out once and for all.

Lysias gathered his troops before Jerusalem and he brought with him a weapon never before seen in Israel, a weapon that his King had promised never to use. General Lysais brought with him a troop of thirty two war-elephants. Lysias and a hundred and twenty thousand men advanced against a small army of Jews led by Judah the Maccabee. As the sun rose Lysias marched his soldiers towards the city. The trumpets sounded and the mighty war-elephants were given wine to drink to make them wild. The thundering of the marching men, the clanking of their armour and the sun glinting on their swords and spears began to frighten the Jewish fighters. And the charge led by the elephants was amazing. It was surprising that the Jews did not run away then and there.

But Judah and his brothers had fought hard for the freedom of the Jewish people and they were not going to give up.

Down from the hills and along the valley came the army of General Lysias. But Judah encouraged his men, and in the attack more than six hundred of the enemy were killed. The Greek soldiers marched on. In front of them were men on horseback and leading the advance were the war-elephants. Each elephant was steered by an expert Indian driver and topped by a wooden castle. This protected the elephant and gave cover to four of the Greeks' toughest fighting men.

It seemed as if the small Jewish army would be destroyed. One of the elephants seemed to be dressed in finer armour and stand taller than the others. Elezar, a brother of Judah the Maccabee, guessed that this must belong to General Lysias or even to the King himself. He decided to attack it.

Eleazar charged alone at the enemy. He swung his sword to left and to right, hacking down Greek soldiers as he ran, until at last he reached the great royal elephant. Here he was the only Jew amongst the host of Greeks. Towering high above him was the angry fighting elephant and on top of it were the Greek Soldiers hurling spears and stones and shooting arrows at him. Eleazar flung himself underneath the elephant and thrust his spear up into its belly with all the strength he had. The animal squealed in pain and began to fall. The driver and the four soldiers were thrown to the ground as the elephant collapsed, crushing Eleazar as it fell.

But instead of encouraging the Jews, Eleazar's death showed them how powerful were the troops of General Lysias, and the retreat began. Judah screamed at his men to attack and his brothers fought bravely, but his soldiers were weak and frightened and began to retreat as the Greeks came on.

Now the King of Syria was only nine years old. General Lysias had put himself in charge of the Empire. News came that another of the King's generals was getting up an army ready to claim the Empire, and Lysias knew that he must leave Israel quickly. Lysias also knew that he must quickly make peace and had to agree that the Jews would no longer be forced to worship the Greek gods. Now they could worship God in the way they had always done. In their moment of defeat God had given the Jews the victory. And so, because of the bravery of the Maccabee brothers, peace was brought to the land once more.

*

Judah made his people famous.
He put on his armour like a giant
and strapped on his weapons of war.
He fought battle after battle
and protected his soldiers with his own sword.

He was like a lion when he fought,
he was like a young lion roaring for food.
He hunted and tracked down law-breakers,
and blasted those who troubled his people.
Law-breakers hid from him in terror,
and evil people were defeated.
Judah led his people to freedom.
Now his name is famous throughout the world,
for he saved a people who were about to be destroyed.

(*from* 1 Maccabees 3:3-6,9)

*

Philo of Alexandria

At the beginning of the Common Era Alexandria, on the Nile delta in Egypt, was a cultured a wealthy city with a population of Greeks and Greek-speaking Jews. After Queen Cleopatra's death (30 BCE) Egypt lost its independence and became a Roman province, a fact bitterly resented especially in the capital Alexandria. The visit by (Herod) Agrippa I (c.10 BCE-44 CE) of Judea provoked attacks against the Jewish inhabitants. The Roman Emperor at the time was Gaius Caesar Germanicus (born 12 CE, ruled 37-41) nicknamed Caligula who was not only mad and erratic, but cruel even by Roman standards. Philo Judaeus (the Jew) (c.20 BCE-c.50 CE) was born of a wealthy well-connected family linked by marriage to Agrippa, which had wide banking interests. Philo himself had a legal training. Although a devout Jew it is probable that Philo knew no Hebrew, the Alexandrian Jews having a thoroughly Greek culture. Philo is noted for the only event in his life whose date is verifiable, his leadership of Alexandrian Jewish delegation to Rome in 40 CE, but chiefly for his theological writings expounding the Jewish faith and heritage for Greeks and for Jews. Fortunately for Philo and his compatriots Caligula was assassinated in 41 CE before he could implement plans for a statue of himself as a god to be installed in the Temple of Jerusalem.

*

Philo and the mad emperor

In the year 40 CE Agrippa, grandson of Herod the Great, passed through the city of Alexandria on his way back to Judea from Rome. The Emperor Caligula, Agrippa's friend, had agreed that Agrippa should be the king of part of Palestine, and Agrippa wanted to share his happiness with the Jews in Alexandria and Egypt where he himself used to live.

The Jews were delighted to see him. They lined the streets and shouted and cheered as if Agrippa was the king of Alexandria too. But in their houses the Greeks muttered and swore. The Greeks were not friends of the Emperor of Rome who ruled them; they were no friends of the Jews either; and there were some Greeks who knew that Agrippa had run away from Alexandria not many years before because he owed them money.

The next day came and now the streets were lined with Greeks cheering and shouting. Through the crowds came a donkey with a scarecrow sitting on it dressed up as King Agrippa but wearing a dunce's cap. And during the weeks that Agrippa spent in Alexandria there were plays in the streets making fun of him, rude songs were sung about him and funny pictures of him were painted on the walls. Agrippa was probably glad to go home.

After Agrippa had gone, however, there were some Greeks who began to realise how stupid they had been. King Agrippa was after all, a friend of the Emperor Caligula; and it was certainly true that Caligula was mad − all the more reason to be worried. Caligula had people whipped if they forgot his birthday and fed his lions with prisoners: what would he do to a city that made fun of one of his friends?

The Greeks decided they must show Caligula what a bad lot the Jews were before King Agrippa could go telling him tales. Someone remembered that the Jews were supposed to have statues of the Emperor as a god in their synagogues. No-one ever bothered to make them − everyone knew what trouble it caused when people interfered with the Jews' religion. Here was a good excuse to get the Jews into trouble.

So the Greeks went to tell the Roman governor Flaccus. He wasn't keen to do anything about it, but he didn't dare upset Emperor Caligula. When stones were thrown through Jewish windows Flaccus did nothing about it. He did nothing when gangs of Greeks went round the streets beating up Jews. There were robberies and murders. But when the Greeks began to drag statues of Emperor Caligula as a god into the Jewish synagogues trouble flared up across the city. There were riots, houses were burned, and people were injured and killed. But still Governor Flaccus stopped his Roman soldiers from doing anything to help the Jews.

A group of Jews met together. One of them was the elderly Philo, a rich lawyer, a man very clever with words. He'd spent many years writing books to explain the Jewish religion to both Jews and Greeks. Now all that seemed wasted as Jews and Greeks fought each other.

'The Greeks say they'll stop attacking us if only we'll put the Emperor's statue in our synagogues,' said one man.

'We've never done it before and we never will. God said we must have no other gods except God himself, and that we must not worship statues,' said another. 'We must send someone to see the Emperor. He may be mad but he'll surely listen to someone like Philo.'

So it was decided that a group of Jews led by Philo should escape from Alexandria and sail across the winter seas to Rome to beg Caligula for justice. But they were followed by a group of Greeks who were keen to make the Jews seem to be the ones who were breaking the law.

In Rome Philo found it impossible to see Caligula. The Emperor did not sit in his palace waiting to hear from people with complaints. He spent his days visiting his luxurious houses in Rome with their parks and gardens planning elaborate alterations. At last Philo tracked him down to a park he owned by the River Tiber, an unhappy place to meet because this was where Caligula enjoyed watching important Romans being put to death.

'So you are the Jews who think that I'm not a god!' sneered Caligula. 'I'll show you who's a god. Just remember this: I can treat anyone exactly as I please.'

Philo didn't need reminding. Everyone knew how Caligula has poisoned his own grandmother, how he'd made his father-in-law cut his own throat with a razor, and many other sickening deeds. Philo tried to explain what was happening in Alexandria, but the Emperor didn't really want to listen.

For some days afterwards Philo was unable to find the mad Emperor. When he did find him again Caligula was staying at another of his great houses on a hill looking down on Rome. He was dressed in women's clothes and wore army boots! With him was one of his government, a Greek from Alexandria, telling him, no doubt, how everything was the Jews' fault.

Caligula was just off to visit another of his expensive houses just around the corner. Philo and the Jews followed trying to get him to listen, knowing that at any minute he might lose his patience and have them thrown off a cliff or torn to pieces by wild animals.

And then Caligula was off to the seaside at Naples. For a joke he had shut all the foodshops in Rome and the starving people were beginning to get angry. He would let the army sort them out while he went on holiday.

Philo and his friends miserably followed him to Naples. They had been in Rome for months and seemed to be getting nowhere. Many of them were frightened and exhausted.

'Be patient and put up with whatever happens. God knows what He's doing,' said Philo. 'Remember that we are not doing this for ourselves, but for our religion.'

'But the man's mad!' said one of the group.

'It's true that people who need to show off like he does all the time are really slaves of their own boasting, however many people they may rule,' said Philo. 'But there is no-one who does not have some goodness inside them.'

And in the end Philo's calm patient arguments with the Emperor paid off. Whether Caligula got tired of seeing the Jews following him around, or whether he really did take notice of the wise elderly Philo, we shall never know. At any rate Caligula said that things should be as they had been before. Philo took that to mean that they did *not* have to have the Emperor's statue in their synagogues, and then rushed back to Alexandria before Caligula changed his mind.

*

Philo is remembered now, not for his brave leadership of the group of Jews who faced the mad Caligula, but for his writings. Some of his work was written to explain the Bible and the Jewish religion to the Greeks in Alexandria; some was written to help Jews living amongst Greeks to understand their own religion.

You should want to be good just for the sake of being good.
(*from* Sobriety 3)

God didn't make anyone who has not got some goodness in him.
(*from* Allegorical Interpretations 1,13)

It's best to trust in God and not in our own dull thoughts and shaky ideas.
(*from* Allegories 3,81)

A wise person thinks of heaven as home and looks on earth as a foreign country.
(*from* Husbandry 14)

Nothing is better than searching for the true God, even if we cannot actually find him with our poor human minds. You will find joy in honestly wanting to learn. Looking, even without finding, is being faithful.
(*from* The Special Laws 1,36-40)

*

The Muslims

The Prophet Salih

The prophet Salih preached sometime during the first millenium BCE to the Thamud people, members of a successful civilisation in the north-west of Arabia. They have left impressive ruins at Al Hijr (also known as Median Salih, the City of Salih) some 300 km north of Medina. Their houses were hollowed out of the cliff with stone-built rooms projecting outwards; over a hundred tombs have been found; and there is a great temple chamber 10 m square by 4 m high carved with pillars and the images of beasts. The Thamud are known to have been polytheistic like other pre-Islamic Arabs.

Salih's message was at first rejected by his own people as was Muhammad's by the Meccans. Muslims believe that many prophets preceded Muhammad, the final prophet. Prophets of Arab tradition, such as Salih, are mentiond, as are prophets of Jewish tradition, such as Noah, Lot, Moses and David, and John the Baptist and Jesus from the New Testament. The prophet Abraham is regarded as the first Muslim and is looked on as the Father of the Arabs as well as of the Jews.

*

The Prophet Salih

Nearly 600 km from Mecca are some strange ruins called Al Hijr. Now the desert sand blows around great lumps of stone were once the great houses, castles and palaces of a rich and mighty people, the Thamud. The Thamud people lived in a land of cool streams, beautiful grassy lawns and flower beds. There grew the finest date palms for many miles around and there should have food and water for everyone.

But the people of Thamud were selfish. The rich were cruel to the poor. They stole from them, they made them work for them and did not let them share in all the good things of Thamud. And, as time went by, the rich became richer and more cruel and the poor became poorer and more miserable.

So God chose Salih to be a prophet to his own people. Salih was an intelligent young man, well-liked by everyone. It was expected that Salih would soon be chosen as one of the leaders of the Thamud.

Everyone was most surprised when Salih began to preach to them. 'Worship only God,' said Salih. 'Share the good things that He has given you. Help the poor people instead of being cruel to them.'

Day after day Salih went round preaching his message, and day by day the rich people grew angrier with him. 'Who do you think you are telling us what to do?' they said. 'We'll worship whatever we want. And well do what we like with the things we own. You're a great disappointment to us, Salih. We thought you were a friend of ours. We hoped you'd become one of our leaders. And now you've really let us down.'

A group of Salih's one-time friends began to plot against him. Nine of them met in secret and planned to kill him by night while he slept. They all swore that they would tell no-one and they waited until the time was right.

Meanwhile Salih went on preaching, but only the poor people listened. One day Salih led a camel into the town. He stood in one of the parks where it could drink the water from the stream and eat the grass. 'This camel shall be a sign,' said Salih. 'If the people have listened to me, they will let the camel eat and drink as it wants. But if they drive the camel away, that will show that they are still cruel and selfish. And God will punish them.'

It wasn't long before the camel was noticed by the Thamud. Angrily they came with sticks and knives and broke the poor camel's legs. And they left it there to die.

'God has given you your chances, and you haven't taken any notice,' said Salih. 'God would forgive you if you were sorry, but none of you care what evil things you do.'

Sadly, Salih left his people. He left them in their beautiful houses with their lovely gardens and rich crops. He left them with their wonderful palaces and their streams and their parks. He left them with their cruelty and meanness and with their plots to kill him. He left them for ever.

Three days later the centre of the town was shaken by a great earthquake. It was so sudden and so hard it was like a thunder blast. Down came the fine houses on to the wicked people. The parks and lawns were ruined and the streams disappeared into cracks in the earth. In minutes the wonderful city was knocked into a pile of ruins and almost everybody was killed. Only the poor people who lived in tiny huts at the edge of the town escaped. The rich, who had had so much and shared none of it, now had nothing at all.

*

The words the prophet Salih spoke to the people of Thamud can be found in the Qur'an, the Holy Book of the Muslims, revealed to the Prophet Muhammad by the Angel Gabriel.

Worship God:
you have no other god but Him.
It is God who made you free from earth
and gave you the earth to live in.
So ask God to forgive you
and turn to Him,
for the Lord is always near
and ready to answer.

(*from the* Holy Qur'an 11: 61)

*

The Companions of the Cave

The meaning of the parable of the Companions of the Cave was revealed to Muhammad in reply to cynics who continually tried to trick the Prophet by their questions and argument. The Christian story of the Seven Sleepers of Ephesus is used to demonstrate how totally man must put his trust in God. Ephesus, in Asia Minor, was a seaport up until Roman times (about 60 km from Ismir in modern Turkey). The Roman emperor Decius (born 201 CE, ruled 249-251) persecuted Christians in his empire. Emperor Theodosius II (born 401, ruled 408-450) was the Byzantine emperor during whose reign the Sleepers awoke. Christianity had been permitted by the Christian Emperor Constantine in 313 CE and made the only state religion under Theodosius II in 380. There is a discrepancy of dates in the old Christian story. The Qur'an mentions no emperor by name and makes the point that it is the meaning of the parable which is important and not the particular emperor involved. The relics of the Sleepers were removed to the Christian church of St Victor in Marseilles, France, where they can still be seen. By name they are Maximian, Malchus, Marcian, Dionysus, John, Serapion, and their dog, Qifmir.

*

The Companions of the Cave

In every town and city throughout the Roman Empire there were many temples and many statues to different gods. Emperor Decius ordered that all the people of the Empire must worship these gods, and had statues of himself put in the temples so that the people would worship him as a god too.

This was some time after Jesus had lived and many people worshipped the One

Almighty God as Jesus had taught. But Decius commanded them all to worship before the Roman statues and he travelled round the Empire making sure they did as they were told.

Emperor Decius came to Ephesus in Turkey. His orders were read out and soldiers sent to all parts of the city to hunt down any followers of Jesus. People were terrified. Children betrayed their parents, and parents betrayed their children. Friends let each other down and people worshipped before gods they didn't believe in.

But there were in Ephesus seven who refused to come to the temples and pray to the Roman statues. They stayed in their own houses praying to God. At last someone betrayed them. They were arrested by the Roman soldiers and brought before the Emperor.

'So you won't worship the Roman gods and you won't bow down before my statue?' said Decius. 'Don't you realise that the punishment is death?'

'We know that,' said Maximian, one of the seven, 'but we worship God and trust him. Death cannot frighten us.'

'Well, we'll soon see,' said Decius laughing. 'I shall be away for a few days. When I come back I'm sure you all will have changed your minds.'

But the seven were determined not to give in to the Emperor's bullying. While he was out of town, they gave away everything they had to the poor people of Ephesus. And then they made their way up to Mount Celion and hid in one of the caves there. After some time they began to get hungry. One of them, Malchus, disguised himself and went down to Ephesus to buy food.

While Malchus was buying bread he heard that Emperor Decius had come back. He had been furious when he had found that the seven had escaped into hiding and he had given orders for them to be captured and brought back to the city to be put to death. Malchus quickly paid for the loaves and hurried back to the cave.

When Malchus gave the news to the friends they were terrified. Malchus made them eat the bread he had brought to give them the strength to face whatever might happen. And they they all prayed to God:

'Oh Lord, give us Your mercy,
And sort out our problems
In the way You think best.'

(*from* The Holy Qur'an 18: 10)

And then they fell asleep.

Meanwhile the people of Ephesus had been questioned by the Emperor, but they could tell him nothing. The seven had given away all they owned and had disappeared. The soldiers searched the town and the countryside but found no trace of them. Finally Decius gave orders for all the caves on Mount Celion to be blocked up. If they had hidden in one of them they would surely starve to death.

Inside the cave the seven sleepers slept on. Years passed and Decius died. No-one was sorry to see him go. Times changed and the Roman gods were worshipped no more. In the towns and cities of the Roman Empire Christian churches were built and people worshipped God without fear. And the seven still slept soundly.

Two hundreds years passed. One day a man from Ephesus was wanting to build a stable and took away the stones that blocked up the cave. One by one the sleepers began to wake. They yawned and stretched and asked one another how long they had slept and what time it was. They all agreed that they had slept throught the night and that it must be the next morning.

However, they felt extremely hungry and once again Malchus volunteered to sneak into Ephesus to buy some more bread. Malchus was puzzled to see a great pile of stones at the mouth of the cave and wondered how they had come to be there. He was surprised when he looked down on Ephesus. It didn't seem to be as he remembered it. And when he came to the city gate and saw above it a Christian cross, he was amazed. 'How could it be?' he wondered. 'Only yesterday Decius was going to kill every Christian he could find, and now the cross of Jesus stands above the city gate.'

Going into the bread shop Malchus asked for some loaves and handed over the money. The baker looked strangely at Malchus with his old-fashioned clothes and his odd way of speaking. And he looked even more strangely at the coins Malchus gave him. They were coins from the time of Emperior Decius over 200 years ago.

The city police were called and Malchus was brought before the governor, frightened for his life.

'This is my own money,' said Malchus, 'and these are my own clothes. I see nothing strange about them.'

'Where do you come from?' asked the governor.

'I am a man of Ephesus,' replied Malchus, and he gave the names and addresses of friends and relations. But no-one had ever heard of them.

'But let me ask something,' begged Malchus. 'Where is Emperor Decius who was so cruel to the followers of Jesus? What on earth happened last night while we slept?'

'There's no emperor by that name,' answered the governor. 'I believe there was many many years ago.'

The bishop was sent for to hear Malchus's strange story. The bishop saw that the hand of God was at work and went up to Mount Celion with Malchus and the governor and a large number of people from Ephesus. And there they found the other six who had slept with Malchus for over 200 years. They were all wearing old-fashioned clothes and spoke in the same strange way as he did. The emperor was called, and all the people worshipped God at the mouth of the cave. Years later a place of worship was built there so that people would remember the power of God and those who put their trust in Him.

*

God!
There is no god but God,
the Everliving, the Everlasting.
He does not slumber nor does He sleep.
All things in heaven and on earth belong to God. . . .
His throne stretches over the heavens
    and the earth,
and He never gets tired of guarding
    and caring for His people.
For He is the Highest and the Most Glorious.

(*from the* Holy Qur'an 2: 255)

*

Ali

Ali was the cousin of the Prophet Muhammad, though much younger, and brought up by him as a son. He became the first male Muslim and spent a great deal of his time very close to the Prophet. He married Fatima, Muhammad's youngest daughter. Ali fought bravely and led the Muslims in a number of battles; he held important positions in the rapidly-expanding Muslim community. After the Prophet's death in 632 CE three caliphs succeeded in turn, followed by Ali in 656 CE, whose caliphate was torn by internal strife among the Muslims, partly over the issue of his appointment. He was born in 602 CE and murdered in 661. Ali and his predecessors are known to most Muslims as 'the Rightly-Guided Caliphs'; a sect sprang up which held that Ali had a prior claim to the caliphate and recognizes the succession through his sons. These Shi'ite Muslims predominate still in Iran today; the rest of the Muslim world are known as Sunnis Muslims.

*

Ali becomes a Muslim

When the Prophet Muhammad was a young boy, both his mother and father had died leaving him alone in the world. Fortunately Muhammad had a kind uncle, Abu Talib, who took him into his own house and treated him like a son of his own.

As the years passed Muhammad became quite wealthy and Abu Talib, who had many children of his own, became old and poor. As Abu Talib had helped Muhammad, now Muhammad helped Abu Talib. He took one of Abu Talib's sons, Ali, to live with him. Muhammad became very fond of Ali and looked after him as if he was a son of his own. But it was not an easy time for Muhammad. He had seen visions of the Angel Gabriel. The angel said Muhammad had been chosen by God to be his Messenger.

Muhammad talked with his family about the things the angel was telling him; Gabriel said that there was only One Almighty God and not many different gods, and that we should worship and praise and thank God for his goodness to us. Muhammad's wife became the first woman to believe him and Ali, aged only ten years old, became the first male to believe.

Muhammad used to take Ali out of the city of Mecca to pray quietly in the desert. One day Muhammad and Ali had washed and said their prayers and were kneeling with their heads touching the ground, when Abu Talib came along. Muhammad explained to Abu Talib that he had been chosen as the Messenger of God and asked him if he would join him in prayer like his young son Ali.

'There's nothing wrong with all our old gods,' said Abu Talib. 'Besides, I'm much too old to jump up and down doing exercises like you two.' So Abu Talib did not become a Muslim. In fact, he never did. But he always helped Muhammad whenever he could, even though he didn't agree with him.

So, for a number of years, Muhammad told only his very close friends and relations about the messages he was hearing from God. They went to their secret place in the desert to pray and they all swore to say nothing to anyone. But then the day came when God told Muhammad that he must begin to preach to all the people. It would not be easy. People would laugh at him. People would even hate him and drive him away. But God had told him to tell the world, and tell the world he must.

Muhammad did not think that he would be able to preach God's word. But for a start he called all his relations together to share a meal with him. Forty of them came and there really did not seem to be enough food to go round. But they all began eating and when the meal was over everyone had eaten as much as he could and there was still food left over.

Muhammad began to get ready to explain what God had told him. But his Uncle Lahab, who must have known what Muhammad was going to do, stood up, said, 'Thank you very much for having us,' and sent everyone home.

Once again Muhammad had to invite everyone to a meal. And this time he stood up quickly when the eating was over, and told them about his messages from God. He said, 'God has told me to tell you. Will you join me? Which of you will help me?'

There was silence. Everyone was embarassed. Nobody wanted to join him, because they thought he must be a bit mad. But nobody wanted to say anything rude to him either, because he had just given them a meal, and he was, after all, a relation of theirs.

But young Ali stood up. 'O Messenger of God!' said Ali, 'I will be your helper!' At the sight of this boy promising to help Muhammad start off a new religion, all the men burst into shouts of laughter. It seemed so ridiculous. And they all went home laughing and chuckling to one another.

But Muhammad began to preach to the people of Mecca and some people listened. They gave up worshipping the stone statues and worshipped the One God with Muhammad. They set their slaves free and gave money to the sick and the poor; and they began to make the other people of Mecca very angry.

People would shout rude things at Muhammad as he walked through the town. People threw things; and it became very hard for the small group of Muslims in Mecca. Muhammad sent most of them to Ethiopia where there was a friendly Christian king, but Muhammad himself, and Ali and one or two others bravely stayed on in Mecca.

But still the leaders of the town were not happy. A group of them met together to plot the death of the Prophet. By night they crept up to the house of Muhammad and surrounded it. And when morning came they rushed in with their knives drawn. Pulling aside the bed-clothes, they found Ali asleep in Muhammad's bed. Someone had told Muhammad of the plot; he had escaped to a friend's house before they came and left the brave young Ali in his place.

The next night Muhammad left Mecca and later journeyed by camel across the desert to the town of Medina where he was welcomed as a great hero.

When it was safe to leave Mecca, Ali came with Muhammad's wife and some friends to live in Medina. They built new homes, found new jobs and new friends and started a new life as Muslims together. But the first thing they did was to start work on the world's first mosque where they could thank God for bringing them to safety.

*

Before the Prophet Muhammad came to Medina there had been many arguments and troubles between the people of the town. But Muhammad brought peace and made them all friends. God offers us his hand in the same way that a rope might be thrown to save people from drowning: we must all work together to save ourselves.

Hold tight, all together,
to the rope which God throws out to you;
And don't argue among yourselves,

but thank God for his goodness to you;
For you were enemies,
and he joined your hearts in love,
so that, by God's grace, you became brothers;
You were on the edge of the fiery pit of Hell,
and He saved you from it.
God shows you these things
so that you will know how to live.

(*from the* Holy Qur'an 3: 103)

*

Abdulla and Bilal

Abdulla ibn Mosood was a slave who had recently been converted to Islam. Opposition to Muhammad's new religion was growing among the influential conservatives in Mecca at this time. Families and tribes dealt severely with members who defected to the new faith. Slaves and other lowly people were dealt with by mob violence. Muhammad taught that the loyalty of the Muslim brotherhood superceded all family or clan ties.

Bilal iba Ribah was the Ethiopian slave of Umaiya ibn Khalaf, one of the wealthiest and most influential members of Muhammad's own tribe. He is known as the first caller to prayer, and his background is important in two respects: the fact that he was a slave shows the appeal of Islam to the poor and oppressed; and secondly, the fact that he was an African demonstrates that, from its beginnings, Islam was a universal religion.

*

Abdulla and Bilal — two brave slaves

The Prophet Muhammad preached to the people of Mecca, but most of them didn't want to listen. He said that the rich should help the poor and the sick: the rich people didn't like that. He said that slavery was wicked; the slaves' masters didn't like that. He preached that there was only One God and not the hundreds of different gods of the Ka'aba temple in Mecca: the people who made money out of the visitors to the Ka'aba didn't like that. But whether people liked it or not, Muhammad kept on preaching.

Muhammad used to have visions of the Angel Gabriel. Gabriel taught Muhammad what God wanted him to know and Muhammad taught his friends. They wrote down what Muhammad told them and collected the writings into the holy book of the Muslims, the Holy Qur'an.

There *were* people who wanted to listen to Muhammad's messages from God. The poor and the sick, the young and the slaves were very interested. Often they would meet in each other's houses and read the Holy Qur'an together. They would learn parts off by heart and talk about how they should live in the way of the new religion of Islam.

Some friends of Muhammad were gathered one day, when one of them said, 'The people of Mecca have heard Muhammad preach, and they have heard what we have said about his messages from God, but they have never actually heard the Qur'an read to them.'

One of the others said, 'Well I wouldn't dare read it to them. They throw stones even at Muhammad.'

Among the friends was a poor slave called Abdulla. 'I'll read it to them,' he said. Everyone was proud of his bravery. It would take a lot of courage to read the Holy Qur'an to people who did not want to hear. 'You wouldn't be safe,' said one man. 'The people of Mecca aren't going to put up with a slave telling them about God. It's been hard enough for Muhammad to do it.'

But Abdulla insisted. The next morning he stood outside the Ka'aba where the people worshipped their many gods. In a brave clear voice Abdulla called out: 'There is only One God, and Muhammad is his Prophet.' And then he recited part of the Qur'an.

The people going to the Ka'aba began to shout at him angrily. When he would not stop, they began to push him, and then kick him and punch him. But Abdulla kept on reciting. They beat him round the face until Abdulla was hurt so badly, and bleeding so much, that he had to stop and go home.

His friends cleaned him up, saying sadly, 'We knew this is what would happen. We warned you not to go.' But Abdulla was full of joy. He smiled happily through the cuts and bruises: 'I spoke the word of God to them,' he said, 'and tomorrow I shall do the same again.'

*

Umaiya ibn Khalaf was a very, very wealthy man and one of the most important men in Mecca. While most people were thin and fit through hard work and not much food, Umaiya was so huge and fat that he had to be helped up from the cushion on which he sprawled. Umaiya was a proud man. He owned houses and land and money and many camels. He would give thanks before one of the hundreds of statues in the Ka'aba when the camels came back safely bringing him even more money. Umaiya had plenty to be pleased about.

Until one day Umaiya found his African slave, Bilal, praying to One God in the way that the Prophet Muhammad had been teaching. Umaiya was furious. He was one of the most important men in Mecca and here was his very own slave following some new religion.

Umaiya ordered Bilal to stop. Bilal refused. Umaiya lost his temper and called for his other slaves to tie Bilal up and stretch him on the burning sand with a large rock on his chest. It was midday and the sun beat down fiercely from the Arabian sky. After some time when Bilal's body ached, his mouth was dry and his head was dizzy, Umaiya waddled out to ask him if he'd give up all this nonsense that Muhammad had been preaching. But all that Bilal would say through his dry cracked lips was, 'There is One God. There is One God.'

Each day after that Umaiya had Bilal the African taken out and left under the blazing sun with that large rock weighing down on his chest. Each day he asked him to give up his silly ideas. But each day Bilal answered, 'There is One God.'

Bilal was beginning to get weak, when one day a friend of Muhammad's passed by. Abu Bakr was a rich mechant and a Muslim. But instead of spending his money making himself comfortable and fat like Umaiya, he spent his money helping the poor and needy. 'Why are you torturing this poor African like this?' asked Abu Rakr.

'It's people like you that have twisted his mind,' replied Umaiya angrily. 'He used to be a good slave, but now all he talks about is worshipping the One God.'

'I have a good strong slave,' said Abu Bakr, 'who does not believe in the One God. Why don't we swap and then we'd both be happy?'

Umaiy looked at Bilal. He was weak now and not much use for anything after all the torture he'd been through, though the look on his face showed his mind was still strong. Umaiya agreed.

As soon as Umaiya and Abu Bakr had swapped slaves, Umaiya sent his new slave off to work, while Abu Bakr set Bilal free to go wherever he pleased.

*

Some years later when the Prophet Muhammad moved with the Muslims to Medina and built the first mosque, Bilal was chosen by the Prophet to call the people to prayer. He called out the same words he had spoken to his cruel master while he was being tortured under the hot sun. He called out the same words that are shouted today and every day from mosques all over the world:

God is greatest.
God is greatest.
God is greatest.
I believe that there is no god but God

and that Muhammad is God's Messenger.
Come to prayers.
Come to prayers.
Come to goodness.
Come to goodness.
God is greatest.
God is greatest.
There is no god but God.

(*from the* Muslim Call to Prayer)

*

Oh believers!
Celebrate the praises of God,
and do this often.
Glorify Him in the morning and in the evening.
It is God who sends you blessings,
who sends the angels,
that He may bring you out of the depths of darkness into the light.
God is full of mercy to people who believe in Him.

(*from the* Holy Qur'an 33: 41-44)

*

Umar

Umar ibn al Khattab was an influential person whom the Muslims won over at a difficult time in their early history. He became as zealous in his spreading of Islam as he had previously been in his persecution of the Meccan Muslims. He was a very tough man and a brilliant ruler, though very simple in his life-style. He was born about 580 CE, converted to Islam in 616 and was appointed by Abu Bakr, Muhammad's temporal successor, as the second caliph in 634 CE. During his rule the Islamic state expanded to include Egypt and part of North Africa, Arabia, western Iran, Iraq and Syria, and that only twenty years after Muhammad's first military success at the Battle of Badr. Umar was assassinated while at prayer in 644 CE.

*

The conversion of Umar

Umar hated the Muslims. He set out for the edge of the town where a meeting of about forty Muslims was being held. At his side hung his sword. As he stamped angrily through the streets of Mecca, he met a friend of his who asked him where he was going in such a bad-tempered hurry.

'I'm going to break up that meeting of Muslims and after that I'm going to kill Muhammad himself,' said Umar.

He was about to carry on his way when his friend caught him by the arm, and said quietly, 'Don't you think you ought to sort out your own family before you interfere with other people?'

'What do you mean by that?' demanded Umar.

'Don't you know that your own sister, Fatima, and her husband, Saeed, have become Muslims?'

Umar marched back through the city streets to his sister's house. He walked straight in and found a slave, who had become a Muslim, reading to them from a scroll which had part of the Holy Qur'an written on it. The slave was terrified. He gave Fatima the scroll and dashed out of the back door.

'I hear you've both become Muslims,' Umar shouted angrily, and he got hold of Saeed ready to hit him. But Fatima threw herself between them. Umar hit his sister across the face.

'Yes, we are Muslims. We believe in One God and that Muhammad is God's Messenger. You can beat us up if you like, but you won't shake our faith.'

Umar saw the blood trickling down his sister's face and felt very ashamed. He asked if he could have a look at the scroll of paper so that he could read what Muhammad had heard from God. But Fatima would not let him touch the scroll of the Holy Qur'an until he had washed as Muslims do. And Umar went out and washed!

When he came back in he took the scroll and read the things that God had revealed to Muhammad. 'What magnificent words!' said Umar.

The slave had been listening to all this and came back in. 'Come now with me to Muhammad,' he said to Umar. 'Become a Muslim like us.' The slave led Umar back through the streets of Mecca towards the edge of the town. Here was the house where the Muslims were holding a meeting. And here was Muhammad.

When the Muslims saw Umar striding down the street towards their house and still wearing his sword, they were ready to bar the door. But Muhammad himself went to the door. 'Umar,' he said, 'when are you going to leave us alone?'

'I have come to be a Muslim,' said Umar quietly. 'I believe that there is only One God and that you are his Messenger.'

Umar was a faithful Muslim who served Muhammad well. Some time after the Prophet's death Umar himself became the leader of the Muslims. The man who had threatened to kill Muhammad helped to spread Islam throughout the world.

*

The scroll that Fatima gave Umar to read was a copy of Chapter twenty of the Holy Qur'an. Most of the chapter tells the story of the Prophet Moses who brought the tribe of Israel from slavery to freedom. Here are the first few verses of the chapter:

> The Qur'an has been revealed by God,
> who created the earth and the heavens on high.
> God, the Most Gracious, is seated on the Throne of the Universe.
> To God belongs
>   all that is in heaven and on earth,
>   all that is under the sky
>   and all that is under the earth.
> Whether you speak aloud or not,
> God knows your secrets and whatever you try to hide.
> God!
> There is no god but God.
> To Him belong the most beautiful names.

(*from the* Holy Qur'an 20: 2-8)

*

The Prophet Muhammad

Muhammad was born in Mecca, Saudi Arabia in 571 CE. He received a revelation from God in 610 and began preaching Islam in public three years later. His message was not well received by the polytheistic Arabs and there was active resistance against the small band of Muslims. Muhammad continued to preach and to receive the revelations of the Holy Qur'an and slowly the number of Muslims grew. In 615 some Muslims were granted protection in Ethiopia by the sympathetic Christian king. In 622 Muhammad organised the emigration to Medina, a town some 400 km north of Mecca. Islam developed here into an organised missionary religion.

The Battle of Bedr in 624 gave a great boost to the young religion; the Battle of Uhud in 625 nearly saw the end of it; while the Battle of the Ditch in 627 pro-ved the turning point and gave the Muslims the confidence to conquer Mecca in 630. Muhammad's Farewell Pilgrimage, which set the traditions for the annual pilgrimages of modern times, took place in 632, the year of his death.

Many prophets taught the message of Islam. The Qur'an names many from the Old and New Testaments as well as some from Arab tradition. Muslims regard Muhammad as the final prophet of God, the culmination of the line of prophets. Muhammad received the complete revelation from God in the form of the Holy Qur'an, the direct word of God to men.

*

Muhammad leaves Mecca

There were some rich people in Mecca who were getting worried about Muhammad. He seemed to them to be a trouble-maker when he talked about One God for all the people, when he talked about freedom for slaves and when he said that the rich must help the poor.

Muhammad was warned to stop preaching. But he could not keep quiet and people still wanted to listen.

Muhammad's enemies began to get nasty. Some of them tortured their slaves who had become Muslims. One man was killed while he was saying his prayers. They shouted rude things and swore at Muhammad as he walked about the town. Muhammad realised that there was not much point in staying in Mecca any longer. He and the Muslims would have to leave.

Plans were made to send the Muslims to Medina. The people there agreed to look after them. In ones and twos and in small groups the Muslims left their homes and friends and families to begin a new life in Medina.

With his friend, Abu Bakr, Muhammad went to stay in a cave outside Mecca. The enemies of Muhammad were furious. Searches were made all around the town. One man even walked right past the cave where they were hiding. But he saw a spider had made its web across the entance and so he thought that no-one could be in there. The rich men in Mecca offered a reward of a hundred camels if anyone could capture Muhammad. But it was no use. The Prophet had escaped.

The Muslims in Medina were very worried about Muhammad. They had heard from Mecca that he had disappeared, but there had been no news since. Every day they would set out in the early morning to stand at the edge of the town. Every day they looked out over the rock and sand at the bare hills and the road from Mecca. But the prophet never came. Every day at noon when the heat was too much to endure and the glare of the sun stopped them from seeing anything, they would go back to their homes.

After noon one day the Muslims had all gone back to the cool shade of their homes when two tired travellers came over the hill and down towards Medina. They stopped for a while in the shade of the first palm tree and were recognised by a man who lived at the edge of the town. 'He has come! He has come!' shouted the man. People ran joyfully from house to house shouting the news. And as Muhammad and Abu Bakr rode towards the centre of Medina crowds of cheering Medinans and happy Muslims waved and laughed for joy.

Wherever he went people came out to ask Muhammad to stay with them. But the prophet said he would let his camel decide. The camel went on until it came to the house of a young man called Khalid ibn Zaid who happened to be a distant cousin of Muhammad's. Khalid gladly invited him to stay.

Abu Bakr noticed an empty barn next to the house and bought it. After a lot of hard work by Muhammad and the Muslims this was to become Muhammad's house and the first Mosque in Medina.

The next few years were not to be years of peace for the Muslims. They had to work hard to make a living and they had to keep fighting off attacks from Mecca. Muhammad had to suffer a great deal from the people of Mecca but the time would come when he would go back there in triumph.

While Muhammad and Abu Bakr were in the cave, Abu Bakr was afraid. After all there were a great many people out hunting for them. 'And there are only two of us,' said Abu Bakr. But Muhammad answered him, 'Have no fear, for God is with us.'

Muslims believe that God is always with us:

God knows all the secrets of heaven and earth;
He is responsible for everything.
So worship him
and put your trust in Him,
for God knows everything that you do.

(*from the* Holy Qur'an 11: 123)

*

Muhammad's battles

The Battle of Badr

Times were hard in Medina. Muhammad and the Muslims had come to live there because the people of Mecca were not interested in the Prophet's message. They were rude and violent towards him. The people of Medina had made Muhammad and the Muslims very welcome, but it meant that everybody had to share work and food and shelter.

In Mecca the leaders were furious about Muhammad's escape, and they continued to make plans to capture him.

A caravan of a thousand camels was on its way to Mecca. The camels carried expensive things bought from all over the world for the merchants of Mecca to sell.The caravan had to pass near to Medina.

The leader of the caravan became worried as they drew near Medina. He was sure that Muhammad would attack and steal all their goods. He sent a message to Mecca asking the leaders there to get an army together to protect the camel caravan.

The messenger raced on ahead to Mecca. He rode into the temple called the Ka'aba in the centre of Mecca and, after making his camel kneel down, he stood on the saddle and called out, 'Help! Help! Muhammad and his Muslims are lying in wait for our camel caravan. They are going to steal everything we have. You will not be in time if you don't hurry. Help! Help!'

People rushed about everywhere looking for their swords and getting their camels ready for battle. In a very short time there was not a man left in the city. An army of a thousand men had set out to attack Muhammad.

When Muhammad heard the news he gathered his own men together. But there were only three hundred of them, some of whom were boys. They had poor weapons and very few horses. But they were brave and Muhammad gave them courage.

The two armies met at Badr just as the sun was rising. Three champions, the best fighters in Mecca challenged the Muslims. Muhammad sent out his uncle Hamza, his cousin Ali and a man called Ubaida. Ubaida was quickly killed but Hamza and Ali won their fights. The Meccans were surprised and shocked that they had been beaten.

And as the battle began the wind whipped up the desert sand in the faces of the Meccans so they could not see. The Muslims came on. Fighting bravely, one man to three Meccans, Muhammad's small army began to win. The prophet shouted encouragement whenever they grew tired and at last the battle was theirs. The enemy escaped back to Mecca, while the Muslim army went joyfully to Medina to tell of their great victory.

*

The Battle of Uhud

After being beaten at Badr, the Meccans spent a year preparing to attack Muhammad again. They were determined not to be defeated a second time so they made up an army of 3000, while Muhammad could only manage 700.

The Meccan army marched towards Medina and camped at the foot of Mount Uhud not far from the town. The people of Medina were frightened by the sight of such a great army and they all argued about what to do. Some said they should go out and attack the enemy, others said they should stay inside the town and defend their houses. For three days they argued.

On the Friday after prayers Muhammad came out of his house dressed in his armour. The crowd had changed its mind again: 'We'll stay inside the city and defend it,' they called.

'We will go out and fight the enemy,' answered Muhammad. 'The Prophet has put on his armour. It is not right that he should take it off without fighting.'

Muhammad led the army of Muslims into position facing the enemy. Every man had his job to do. The captain of the archers was told to guard the side of the army in case the Meccan horsemen should attack.

The battle began and everything went the Muslims' way. Although Muhammad's uncle Hamza was killed, victory seemed to be near. The army started to move forward chasing the enemy. The archers began to follow.

'Come back!' shouted their captain. 'Stay in your positions!' But they took no notice. The commander of the Meccan horsemen soon noticed, however, that one side of the Muslim army was not protected and he ordered his men to charge.

Two hundred horsemen swept from behind the Muslim army, scattering the archers. The horsemen came upon the Prophet himself. One horseman killed the man who was carrying Muhammad's flag and the shout went up that Muhammad was dead. Many Muslims began to run when they heard this.

The enemy attacked the group where Muhammad was. A stone hit Muhammad's mouth and knocked out a tooth. The blow of a sword hit his helmet cutting it into his head. But Ali was there and Abu Bakr and the small group defended itself bravely.

The Meccans had scattered the Muslim army and they thought they had killed

Muhammad so they left the battle and made for home. It had been a terrible day for the Muslims but the Battle of Uhud taught them a lesson that they never forgot.

*

The Battle of the Ditch

The Meccans planned to attack Medina again. They knew that they should have destroyed the city after the Battle of Uhud and that they had missed their chance. For two years they stored up weapons and talked to other tribes hoping to get them to join in. At last they were ready.

An army of 10 000 men left Mecca and set out towards Medina. Muhammad's spies brought the news to the Prophet. The Muslims had nearly lost the Battle of Uhud when they had gone out to fight the enemy outside the city. This time Muhammad decided that they would stay inside the city and defend it.

One of the Muslims, Salman, had come from Iran and he had seen the great battles between the Roman and the Persian Empires. He suggested that they dig trenches round Medina to stop the enemy from getting near enough to fight properly. Muhammad agreed.

The Prophet himself marked out the places to dig and he joined in the digging with the other Muslims. Every day for twenty days they worked in the cold winter wind and the trenches were only just finished when the ten thousand soldiers from Mecca began to arrive.

An enormous cloud of dust was thrown up by the huge army. They were so many that they seemed to be coming from every direction. By the time they had set up their camp it was late evening and the town of Medina was completely surrounded.

Muhammad had only three thousand soldiers to fight for him, but the Meccans could not reach them. They had never seen ditches before and had no way of crossing over them. Showers of arrows were fired across from time to time but they were too far away to do any harm. Sometimes the Meccans tried to cross the trenches, but they were too wide and deep, and the Muslims soon sent them hurrying back to safety.

For thirty days the Meccans waited and for thirty days nothing happened. They were running out of food for themselves and for their camels and horses. The enemy were desperate for something to happen.

One day four Meccans galloped hard towards the ditch and with a great leap jumped across to the other side. The leader challenged Muhammad to send out his best fighter to battle against him. Muhammad's cousin, Ali, wanted to go. Ali was given Muhammad's own armour and sword.

The man from Mecca climbed down from his horse as Ali came forward. They circled around one another and then, with a rush, their swords met. They fought so fiercely that they could not be seen behind the cloud of dust. But when the dust settled, Ali stood there, his enemy dead at his feet. The Muslims raised a great cheer, while the three Meccan horsemen galloped quickly back to their camp.

A month had passed and the ten thousand Meccans had not been able to make Muhammad give up. A sudden cold wind blew up. Thunder and heavy rain sent the Meccans running to their tents. Horses and camels were frightened and began to stampede, sending tents and men flying. There was nothing the Meccans could do. They were fed-up and frightened. They just wanted to go home. And go home they did.

The Muslims in Medina led by Muhammad gave thanks to God.

*

Muslims believe that without God's help at the Battle of Badr they would have been beaten. They were outnumbered three to one. But they were fighting for God and the Meccans were fighting against Him.

> God has given you a sign in the two armies
>   that fought against each other.
> One was fighting for God,
> the other was fighting against God
>   and there were twice as many of them.
> But God helps whom He wants to help.
> There is a warning here
>   for people who have eyes to see.

(*from the* Holy Qur'an 3: 13)

At the Battle of Uhud the archers did not obey orders and left their positions. The battle was nearly a disaster. But God always helps people who put their trust in Him.

> God gave you a message of hope
>   to give courage to your hearts.
> There is no help except from God,
>   The Most High, the Most Wise.

> To God belongs everything in Heaven and on earth.
> He forgives whom he wants.
> And punishes whom he wants.
> But God is very forgiving and most merciful.

(*from the* Holy Qur'an 3: 126-127)

The lesson for Muslims to learn from the battles is that they must put their trust only in God.

Running away will not do you any good
  if you are running away from death.
. . .
Who can protect you from God
  if He wants to punish you
  or if He wants to give you mercy?
You will find no protector or helper
besides God.

(*from the* Holy Qur'an 33: 16-17)

*

Muhammad's farewell pilgrimage

One night in Mecca a tribe of non-Muslims attacked a Muslim tribe while they were asleep. Some of the Muslims escaped to find safety in the temple of the Ka'aba. The Meccans took no notice of their being in the Ka'aba and murdered them all as they begged for mercy.

Muhammad could not allow this treatment of his followers and sent a message from Medina that the Meccans must pay a fine to the families of the murdered tribe. The Meccans refused. Muhammad called for volunteers to come to Mecca with him. Over 10 000 men volunteered.

The Muslim army set out for Mecca. The Meccans were terrified. They had a poor army and all their best soldiers had become Muslims. After all the nasty things they had said and done to Muhammad, what would the Prophet do now he had grown so powerful?

The army marched into Mecca while the people hid in their houses. Muhammad rode his camel to the centre of the temple of the Ka'aba and called the Meccans to him.

'There is no god but God alone,' he announced, and he ordered the many statues of Arab gods to be destroyed. 'What shall I do with you now?' asked Muhammad. The people thought of their own cruelty and wickedness. Muhammad said, 'Go. You are free. This is a day when your past sins are forgotten. God has forgiven you.'

Muhammad was powerful enough to destroy the city and the people, but he was a man of peace and it was peace he brought to Mecca.

*

Muhammad came back to Mecca on pilgrimage the year after that and finally the year after that. This last pilgrimage is called the Farewell Pilgrimage.

120 000 Muslims had come to Mecca for the pilgrimage. Muhammad sat on

his camel on a great stretch of flat land outside the city and spoke to them.

'Listen carefully to what I have to say, because I don't know whether we shall meet again. Just as this day and this city is holy, so you must look on the life of every Muslim as holy. All Muslims are brothers; none is greater than any other except in worshipping God. Listen to my words. I leave you two things: the Holy Qur'an and the example of my life. Follow these and you cannot go wrong.'

The people listened to these and other words spoken by the Prophet and followed him as he walked around the Ka'aba seven times. He did things at Mecca that millions of Muslims have done down the years ever since and still do today.

Muhammad left Mecca that year never to come back again.

*

Three months later Muhammad fell ill. And after some days of illness he died. His last words were: 'Lord, forgive me. Now the Best Friend is in Heaven.'

Umar was so upset he could hardly control himself. He rushed out of the house and threatened to kill anyone who said that Muhammad was dead. A crowd began to gather to listen to him.

Abu Bakr, Muhammad's closest friend, came back to find Umar shouting madly at the crowd. He gently tried to calm him down, but Umar did not even notice him. Abu Bakr went and stood some way away and quietly called the people to him.

'If anyone here worships Muhammad, they should know that now he is dead. But anyone who worships God should know that God is alive and shall live for evermore.'

Sad though it was that the Prophet had died, Muhammad was a man and men die. But the way that he lived is still there for all to see, and the Holy Qur'an given to him by God is still there for all to read.

The last complete chapter of the Qur'an to be revealed to Muhammad by the Angel Gabriel is called 'help' and tells of the people who were hurrying to become Muslims.

In the Name of God,
the Most Gracious, the Most Merciful.

When God helps you
  and brings you victory,
and when you see people coming in crowds
  to God's religion,
sing praises to the Lord
  and pray for His forgiveness,
for God is Most Gracious,
  Most Merciful.

(*from the* Holy Qur'an 110)

*

The Sikhs

Guru Nanak

Nanak was born in Talwandi in the Punjab (now Pakistan) in 1469 CE of a high-caste well-to-do Hindu family with high material ambitions for him. Nanak, however, showed a growing interest in religion and in caring for the poor. He lived in a society of Hindus and Muslims and at the age of 20 had a revelation of the presence of God after which he preached that empty religious practices and differences among men are meaningless compared with true worship of the One God for all men. He made a number of missionary journeys particularly in the Punjab but as far apart as Sri Lanka, Tibet and Mecca, and set up religious communities as he went. He made his home the village of Kartapur which became the focus of the Sikh community. He died in 1539 CE having founded a new religion rather than reconciling Hinduism and Islam and leaving a wealth of writings now to be found in the Guru Granth Sahib, the Sikhs' holy book, which express his rejection of convention and ritual and emphasise that union with God will end the transmigration of the soul by the realisation of His Word.

No Hindu, no Muslim

Nanak was brought up in the Punjab 500 years ago where there were many Muslims and many Hindus. Nanak himself was a Hindu but he had many Muslim friends and knew as much about their religion as he did about his own. Nanak spent many hours as a boy and as a young man thinking about what God must be like and what should be the right way to worship Him.

One day Nanak disappeared. He had last been seen near the river and everybody thought that he must have drowned. But three days later he reappeared. 'I have been with God,' he said.

No-one knew quite what he meant. Nanak told them: 'There is no Hindu. There is no Muslim. I am a brother to all lovers of God. All lovers of God are brothers together.'

Hindus and Muslims were shocked at what he said and Nanak was called before the local governor, Daulat Khan.

'What do you mean saying that there is no Hindu and Muslim?' asked the governor. 'We're Muslims, aren't we? We say our prayers five times a day.'

'It's very difficult to be a good Muslim,' answered Nanak. 'But you don't understand what I mean. You think that being a Muslim or a Hindu is the most important thing. But the most important thing is to love God and worship Him. We are all sons and daughters of God; we are all brothers and sisters.'

As Nanak was trying to explain what he meant to Daulat Khan, the call to prayer could be heard coming from the village mosque.

'If that's what you think,' said Daulat Khan, 'why don't you come and pray with us at the mosque?'

'I am happy to worship God at any time,' replied Nanak, and they went to the mosque. They took off their shoes and washed and then went in. Daulat Khan bowed and knelt and said the prayers with the other Muslims there. But Nanak just stood still.

'You said that you would pray with us,' said Daulat Khan angrily after prayers were over. 'You just stood there doing nothing!'

'I would have prayed with you,' said Nanak, 'if you had been praying. But your mind wasn't on God at all. You were saying the right words but you were actually thinking about other things.'

It was true. Daulat Khan had been thinking of a deal he was making for buying horses. He promised to think about what he was saying to God in future.

*

In many of his writings Guru Nanak teaches that you must mean what you say when you pray to God and that you must understand the ways in which you worship. The important thing is to praise God in an honest way.

Know God Who creates and destroys the world;
know Him by the things he has made.
Do not search for the True One far away,
but understand that His Word is in every heart.
God is the True Word, the creator of the universe;
do not imagine that He is far away.
You will find peace by meditating on the Name of God;
without God's Name the game of life is lost.

(*from* Vadahamsu Alahani 4 *of the* Guru Granth Sahib)

*

Guru Nanak and the thief

Guru Nanak was the first leader of the Sikhs. He lived in India at a time when there was some bad feeling between Hindus and Muslims and tried to make people from both religions realise that they were all children of God. Sometimes people would ask him whether he was a Hindu or a Muslim. He would answer, 'I am neither. I am a friend to all lovers of God.'

Guru Nanak travelled many thousands of miles around India and the countries nearby trying to make people understand that it is no use just saying your prayers, it's no use just going to the temple or the mosque, it's no use just performing ceremonies or going to holy places on pilgrimage, it's not even any use doing good things, if you do not love God. On his travels he would take his friend, Mardana. Mardana was a rebeck player (a rebeck is a stringed bowed instrument) and the two of them would play and sing hymns of praise to the people they visited.

On one journey Guru Nanak and Mardana came to the town of Tolumba. Here there was a fine house and at the gates stood a very holy-looking man. He was dressed all in white, around his neck he wore a rosary, a necklace of Muslim prayer-beads, and on his forehead he had painted the mark of a Hindu saint.

'Welcome, travellers,' said the man. 'My name is Sajjan. I am a friend to Hindus and to Muslims and so I have turned my house into a temple and a mosque so that Hindus and Muslims may both pray here.'

Sajjan invited Nanak and Mardana to pray and told them they were welcome to stay there for the night.

But Guru Nanak had seen into his heart and knew that everything was not as it seemed to be. In fact, Sajjan was a thief and a murderer. And his house was not a place where Hindus and Muslims could pray, nor was it a safe place to stay for the night. His house was a trap. He would welcome travellers and invite them to stay with him. And he would kill them while they slept and steal all they had. In this way Sajjan had built himself a large and comfortable house and lived a life of luxury.

Sajjan had food brought for Nanak and Mardana and after they had eaten Sajjan sat and listened as Mardana began to play and Nanak began to sing one of his hymns praising God. Perhaps it was this one:

O God,
You are mysterious and beyond our understanding;
You are greater than words can say,
You are everlasting;
Have mercy upon me!
O God,
You are everywhere in the universe,
and Your light shines in every heart.
(*from* Bilavalu 2 *of the* Guru Granth Sahib)

And as Mardana's music began to fill the evening air, Guru Nanak's words began to fill Sajjan's heart and tears filled his eyes. Sajjan realised what his life of wicked selfishness meant and he was truly sorry for the things he had done.

From that time Sajjan's house really did become a place where travellers could rest and where holy people of any religion could say their prayers to God.

*

Guru Nanak's sons

Guru Nanak became famous for his teachings and wherever he went people would come from villages and towns to hear him speak. He taught them of the magnificence of God and how we should love and praise Him. He sang hymns and said prayers and the people joined in. But although he was so famous that people would travel for miles to come and see him, he never grew big-headed or proud. He led a very simple life with no fine clothes or fancy food and certainly no servants. He grew all the things his family needed on their own small farm and he worked in the fields like any other villager.

But as the Guru began to get old (he was nearly 70 now), he began to worry about who should lead the Sikhs when he died. He had many faithful followers to choose from; but it would take more than just being faithful to be the next Sikh guru. He had two sons of his own; but just being his son was not enough to be the next guru.

Of the Sikhs who had come to live in the Guru's village Nanak loved Lehna more than most. Lehna had given up everything to live near the Guru so that he could hear him preach every day. Lehna was quiet and honest and hard-working.

Guru Nanak had been out in the fields one day cutting grass for the cows to eat. He had tied the grass up to make three great bundles of hay which now had to be carried back to the house. Nanak was tired and aching and looked round for someone to help him, but all the other workers had gone home.

'Please carry these bundles of hay for me,' said Nanak to his eldest son.

'But, Father, the grass is muddy and wet and it will ruin our best clothes. There's probably someone around who would carry it for you.'

Guru Nanak asked his younger son.

'But, Father, heavy work like that is not for us. We are the sons of the Guru. Couldn't a servant or one of the workers do it?'

Into the field came Lehna. 'I shall be a servant and a worker for the Guru,' he said. And he picked up all three heavy dirty bundles and took them back to the house.

And so it was many times. Lehna showed that he was willing to do whatever work the Guru had for him, and Nanak's own sons were not. Guru Nanak called all his people together and announced to them that Lehna would be the next guru.

*

Guru Nanak was a friend to Muslims and Hindus alike. He told them that they should not waste time arguing who was best, but should get on with it and worship God.

And just before he died a group of Hindus and a group of Muslims began to claim him for their own. Each said that they wanted to give him a funeral in their own way. Hindus burn a dead body and scatter the ashes in a river, while Muslims wrap the body in a white sheet and bury it.

Guru Nanak himself settled the argument. As he felt that death was coming near he lay down. 'Let the Hindus put flowers on my right. Let the Muslims put flowers on my left. Whoever's flowers are still fresh in the morning may give me the funeral they want.'

Nanak pulled a sheet over himself and died peacefully.

The next morning the Hindus and Muslims woke early to find that both lots of flowers were still bright and fresh. But Guru Nanak's body had gone!

*

Guru Nanak died peacefully and happily because he had complete faith in God. Although God is greater than anyone can imagine, Guru Nanak believed that He is very close to us.

> Beyond our understanding, infinite, out of reach and out of our sight; free from death and sin, with no race or colour, never born but created by Himself; not loving wordly things and having no doubts or worries; I sacrifice myself to You, O God, the absolute Truth. You have no shape or colour or body at all, but You reveal Yourself to us in your True Word.

(*from* Sorathi 6, *of the* Guru Granth Sahib)

Guru Angad

Angad was born in 1504 CE of a devout Hindu family in the Punjab in northern India. His life was changed by a meeting with Guru Nanak who was preaching at a Hindu pilgrimage attended by Angad's family. He left the family business to join Nanak's Sikh community and was so dedicated and pious that the Guru changed Lehna's name (as it had been formerly) to Angad (which means Myself). Angad succeeded to the guruship in 1539 in preference to Nanak's own sons who had been considered unworthy by their father. His life's work consisted of re-emphasising the message of the first guru and in consolidating the institutions he had set up: he adapted the Gurm khi alphbet to write down Nanak's hymns which were in the vernacular and not in the classical Sanskrit of the Hindus; he continued to establish Sikh communities with free kitchens where all castes would be served; and he demonstrated by his personal example that Sikhs should live their lives as ordinary householders working for an honest living. He died in 1552 CE.

*

Guru Angad and two big-headed musicians

In the village where Guru Angad lived were two wonderful musicians. They played their instruments and sang when the Sikhs were gathered together and all the people were happy to join in or just listen.

But as Guru Angad grew more famous throughout India and more and more people came to see him and hear him speak the two musicians began to grow more proud and boastful.

'It's true, isn't it, friend,' said Balwand, one of the musicians, 'that there wouldn't be half so many people here if it wasn't for our beautiful playing.'

'It is true,' said Satta, the other musician. 'The Guru speaks well but the people travel from miles around to hear us play.'

An old Sikh had come to the village to listen to Angad preach. 'I have heard what excellent musicians you are,' said the Sikh. 'Would you sing a hymn for me listen to, please?'

'Certainly not,' answered Balwand. 'We are the Guru's musicians.'

'Indeed no,' said Satta. 'We're not going to sing hymns for peasants like you.'

The Guru came to hear of this, and that evening as the Sikhs gathered to hear Angad preach and to sing praises to God, the two musicians got ready to play. They sat in front of Guru Angad and began. As they started to sing the Guru turned round so that his back was towards them. Balwand and Satta were rather annoyed and they moved round in front of him again. Angad turned round to face the opposite way. Wherever they stood the Guru would not look at them. At last they asked him what was the matter.

'If you will not sing to one of my Sikhs,' replied Angad, 'then you must not sing to me either.'

They got down on their knees before him, ashamed in front of the crowd and they begged him to forgive them. Of course, Angad was happy to do this.

Unfortunately Balwand and Satta did not stay humble for long. They decided that they would continue to play for the Guru but they wanted higher wages and they were determined to get them.

Balwand went to Guru Angad and told him that one of his daughters was going to get married soon. This would be an expensive business, he said, and he would need at least 500 rupees to pay for it.

Guru Angad did not have that kind of money, but he said he would get it for them by the New year if they could wait a couple of months.

'We can't wait as long as that,' said Balwand rather haughtily. 'I'm afraid we need the money right now. Can't you borrow some money to give us?'

'No. I'm sorry,' said Angad. 'Borrowing is a bad thing. Just be patient and leave things in God's hands.'

'Look!' said Balwand getting cross. 'If it wasn't for our wonderful playing and singing nobody would come to hear you preach at all. It's us that have made you famous. If you won't pay us the money we'll go home and sing there.'

And go home they did.

And at home they played and they sang but no-one came. The Sikhs still went to hear Guru Angad. Angad sent messengers to encourage the musicians to come back, but they were too proud and stayed at home.

Angad found some other Sikhs who could play and sing. They really weren't very good at first, but Angad believed that God was interested in how well you mean the words you sing and not how well you sing them. And with practice they got better.

Angad sent another messenger to bring the musicians back, but they were rude to the messenger, they were rude about Angad and his new musicians, and they were rude about Guru Nanak. They even said that Guru Nanak would never have been famous if it hadn't been for his good musicians. This insult to the first leader of the Sikhs was too much for Angad. 'If ever I hear of anyone speak well of Balwand and Satta again, I shall have his beard shaved, his hair cut off and ride him sitting backwards on a donkey in disgrace around the village. Never mention their names again!'

The two musicians sat at home lonely and miserable. They sent messages now to Guru Angad but he took no notice. At last they called on a Sikh who was known to be a good friend of Angad's. Perhaps he could get the Guru to forgive them.

Ladha knew how angry Angad must be. And he knew that he meant what he said, but he felt sorry for the two musicians and decided he must help them. He shaved off his fine beard and had his long hair cut and he rode sitting backwards on a donkey all round the village where Angad lived. It was as if Ladha himself was in disgrace. He came to the door of the Guru's house and begged forgiveness for Balwand and Satta. When the Guru saw that Ladha was prepared to suffer the shame and embarrassment of the two musicians his heart was softened and he forgave them for Ladha's sake.

Guru Angad called Balwand and Satta to him. They were full of thanks but so shame-faced they could not look their Guru in the eye and fell at his feet. Angad put their instruments in their hands and told them to play as they had never played before – not for themselves, not even for him, but for the glory of God.

Why praise the things that God has made?
Praise only God who has made them!
There is no giver of gifts but the One God.
Praise the Creator who made the world;
Praise the Giver who gives all gifts.
Only God who has everything is everlasting;
Glorify and praise the Lord who has no beginning or end.

(*from* Sarang ki War *by* Guru Angad *in the* Guru Granth Sahib)

*

Guru Amar Das

The third Sikh guru was born in 1479 CE, succeeded as guru in 1609 and died in 1574 at the age of 95. During his guruship it became clear that Sikhism was a distinct religion and neither a Muslim nor Hindu sect. Amar Das organised the growing following into local communities in the charge of ministers answerable to him. He had the first Sikh place of pilgrimage built; Sikhs had used Hindu shrines previously. And he instituted specifically Sikh ceremonies of birth, marriage and death. His friendship with the Muslim Emperor Akhbar lent respectability to the religion and people from the higher castes began to join the Sikhs; previously the membership consisted largely of the poor, the disenfranchised and the untouchable for whom Sikhism offered hope. This further delineation of the Sikh religion was storing up trouble for the future, however, as the priestly Hindu class grew concerned about the effect this was having on their adherents.

Guru Amar Das and the lame man

Some way from the village where Guru Amar Das lived was the house of a lame man called Prema. Prema was able to walk with the help of a crutch though he was slow and awkward and it took him a long time to get anywhere. Prema was a Sikh and one of the duties he enjoyed was to take a large jug of milk every morning to the village of the Guru. The Guru would drink some of the milk himself and share the rest between the people of the village. And Prema would begin the slow journey home.

It was the rainy season in India. Rain had fallen in torrents over the past few days and the roads were like steaming rivers of mud. It was almost impossible for anyone to travel anywhere.

But that morning the chief man of the village stepped out of his door to see Prema struggling through the mud with his crutch to support him in one hand and the great jug of milk in the other. 'You can't go out on a day like this,' said the chief man. 'You'll fall over and injure yourself.'

Another villager shouted across from his doorway: 'Why don't you ask your guru to mend your leg. If he can't even heal a lame leg how on earth is he going to save you when you die?'

Prema kept calm and told them that he had a job he must do for the guru and said that he did not become a Sikh to have his bad leg healed. Prema struggled on his way.

When he finally arrived at the Guru's village covered in mud and exhausted he happened to tell Amar Das of the things that had been said to him at his own village. 'Your leg shall be made better,' replied Amar Das. 'Go to see Husaini Shah is his hut by the river. Tell him I have sent you to be cured.'

Husaini Shah was a Muslim holy man who lived quite alone by the river. He spent his days praising God and would chase anyone with a stick who came to disturb his peace and quietness. But, as the Guru had told him, Prema went to see Husaini Shah.

As Prema came near to where Husaini Shah lived he called out who he was and told him that Guru Amar Das had sent him. Husaini Shah said he could sit by him for a minute but only because the Guru had sent him. Prema told his story. And as he finished Husaini Shah picked up a stick: 'Now go away,' he shouted. 'You've come here wasting my time about bad legs and walking through the mud? Go on! Go away!'

Prema was terrified of what this angry holy man might do. He jumped up and began to run as fast as he could. He had got some way before he realised that he had left his crutch by the river. Prema could walk properly again!

Prema was so happy that he came back to Husaini Shah to thank him. 'It was nothing to do with me,' said the holy man. 'Your leg was healed when the Guru sent you to me. Now go back and kneel before him. There are many holy men like me, but there is only one Guru.'

When springtime comes life in nature is born again and grows again. Guru Amur Das wrote this hymn saying that God is like the springtime, that he causes people to be be born again by the love in their hearts.

When spring comes, the forest blooms; But men and animals bloom only by thinking on God; In this way their minds are refreshed. By thinking on God's name day and night in the way that the Guru has taught you your pride will be removed and washed away. When the true Guru reads out his poems and sings his hymns the whole world will bloom again by his love. Fruits and flowers appear when God makes them appear; When a man finds the true Guru, he finds God who is the root of all things. God is the springtime and the world is his garden.

(*from* Ramkali ki War 1 *of the* Guru Granth Sahib)

Guru Ram Das

Ram Das was born as Jetha in the city of Lahore (now in Pakistan) in 1534 CE. His parents were religious people but very poor. They both died while he was young. At the age of twelve Ram Das joined the Sikh community and went to live in the service of Guru Amar Das at Goindwal. Such was his devotion to duty and his aptitude for understanding that the third Guru passed the succession on to him in 1574. Some years previously Ram Das had married Bibi Bhani, the Guru's daughter. Ram Das's most memorable achievement was the foundation of the city of Amritsar in 1577. He had the great pool, the Tank of Nectar, after which the city is named, excavated by volunteers. During the construction living accommodation was set up and traders were attracted to the site which stands in the middle of fertile agricultural land and near the crossing of trade routes. The city prospered and became the holy city of the Sikhs. The Golden Temple and its Tank of Nectar are visited by Sikhs from all over the world. Ram Das died in 1581.

Guru Ram Das

There lived in the great city of Lahore a little boy called Jetha. Jetha was strong and cheerful and handsome, but his parents were desperately poor. However, both his mother and his father came from good families of good tribes and they had great ideas for their son. They wanted him to do well, to make money and to become rich and important. And so, although they were religious people themselves, they were rather disappointed that Jetha should want to spend all his time talking to the holy men who passed by on their way through the city. These holy men had given up money and owned nothing but the poor clothes they had on. Jetha wouldn't become rich by talking to them.

Not far from Jetha's poor house lived a woman who boiled beans. Every day she packed them in baskets to take around the city to sell. She did not make much money doing this but she earned enough to live on. One day Jetha suggested to his mother that they should do the same thing. His mother was delighted – her son was going to make them some money. Jetha's mother prepared the beans that night and in the morning put them into a basket for Jetha to sell.

Next morning early Jetha set out with his basket of boiled beans. He made his way towards the busy city streets and the market places. But as he passed by the River Ravi he saw a group of holy men at their morning prayers. They had nothing at all and yet they were cheerful. They had no clothes but the ones they were wearing, they had no money, and they didn't even know if any kind person was going to give them food that day. And yet there they were praising God at the tops of their voices. After the holy men had finished their prayers and bathed in the river Jetha went up to them and offered them the boiled beans he had for sale. But he wanted no money for them. He gave them to the holy men for nothing.

When the holy men had eaten and the basket was empty they thanked him and blessed him and promised him that God had seen the kind thing he had done and that God would reward him in his own way.

Jetha's family remained as poor as ever. When he was only seven his mother died. His father too died some time later. What worse could happen? What could God's reward be?

Jetha was twelve years old when a group of Sikh men and women came through the city of Lahore where he lived with his grandmother. The Sikhs were singing and dancing, playing on drums and cymbals and their happiness was noticed by everyone they passed.

'Where are you going?' asked Jetha running out into the street.

'We're going to see Guru Amar Das, the leader of Sikhs,' replied one of them. 'Come with us!'

And Jetha did. He had nothing to stay in Lahore for. Jetha and the group of Sikhs travelled to the village where Guru Amar lived. As they entered the village Jetha could feel the difference. Instead of the noise and chaos of Lahore, the city of the very rich and the very very poor, here was a village where there was work for everyone. The work was hard but everyone enjoyed it. Here was a village full of people busy doing jobs, but full of peace and joy. And at the centre of the village was Guru Amar Das, leader of the Sikhs.

In the evenings after work the Sikhs would gather to hear the Guru preach about loving God. Hymns would be sung about God's love for men and prayers would be said.

Guru Amar Das asked Jetha about himself and he asked him why he had come. Jetha told his story, saying, 'I could find no happiness in Lahore. I have come here to find God's reward for me.'

'Work hard for other people and you shall have God's reward,' answered the Guru.

From that day Jetha never stopped working. He was up as early as anyone fetching water, bringing firewood, cooking, washing, cleaning, sweeping, digging, weeding, doing all the jobs around the Guru's village that needed to be done. But as hard as Jetha worked, he never felt tired. He never grew miserable, but seemed to be happier the harder he worked. God had rewarded Jetha's work for others with the gift of happiness.

Guru Amar Das told him that by helping others he was working for God. his name should be Ram Das which means 'The Servant of God'. And as the years went by Amar Das realised that Jetha, or Ram Das was the only servant of God who was good enough to be the guru of the Sikhs after he had died. It was not until the boy Jetha had grown up to be the 40 year old Ram Das with a wife and family that Guru Amar Das died. But when he did Jetha became Guru Ram Das, the fourth Guru and leader of the Sikhs.

Many Sikh hymns talk about the importance of saying God's name. This is not meant to be recited as a sort of magic spell, but as a reminder always of the greatness of God and the plan that He has for his people. Guru Ram Das wrote this hymn:

Have mercy on me, O God, and open my heart
    So that I may think on your Name day and night.
God is all comfort, all excellence, and all richness;
    by saying God's name you will not suffer misery

or hunger.
O my soul, God's name is my brother and friend.
Let me follow the Guru's teaching;
Let me sing the praises of God's name;
At my last hour it will help me and bring me to God.

(*from the* Gujari, *of the* Guru Granth Sahib)

Guru Arjan

Arjan was the son of Ram Das and the first of the gurus to be born a Sikh. He was born in 1563 CE and succeeded as the fifth Guru in 1580 in preference to his two older brothers, one of whom was to spend his life conniving against Arjan. Arjan completed the construction of the Tank of Nectar at Amritsar and laid the foundation stone of the Golden Temple there on the place where his father used to meditate. He compiled the Adi Granth, the Sikh holy book, from the writings of the earlier Gurus and from writings by Muslim and Hindu saints. This book containing about 6000 hymns was placed at the centre of the Golden Temple. Guru Arjan was arrested by Emperor Jehangir whose liberal father, Emperor Akhbar had died in 1605. Jehangir saw it as his mission to convert his subjects to Islam and he apparently used whatever means were necessary. Arjan was accused of treason, conspiring with enemies of the state. He was cruelly tortured and executed in 1606 to become the first Sikh martyr.

Guru Arjan and the selfish village

Guru Arjan travelled around preaching to the people. Sometimes they listened and sometimes they walked away, but Arjan preached to them anyway. He told them of the greatness of God and tried to show them that prayers and hymns and going to the temple or the mosque are no good at all unless you open your hearts to God's love.

One day Arjan came to a village called Khanpur not very far from his home town. Here Arjan stopped with the friends who were with him. They prayed and sang hymns and sat quietly thinking about God until the evening.

But as the sun went down, the clouds came over. It began to grow cold and first it drizzled and then it poured down with rain. 'Let's ask someone in the village for shelter,' said one of the Guru's friends. 'There are some big houses here.'

'I'm afraid that just because the houses are big does not mean the people are kind,' answered Arjan. 'We'd be better off sheltering under a tree or something.'

But the Guru's friends were wet and cold and he decided to ask for shelter for their sakes. Coming up to the first large house Arjan knocked on the door to ask for shelter. 'Anywhere will do,' he said. 'The stable or one of the outhouses would be fine.'

'Go away!' shouted the man who answered the door. 'We don't want tramps round here.'

The Guru tried another house. And another. The reply was always the same: 'Go away! We don't want you here.'

But in the village tucked out of sight behind the larger houses was a small hut. It was made out of sticks and straw, it leaked a little and the wind blew through the cracks. But it was the home of a poor man called Hema. Hema made a living by grinding corn on a handmill for the rich people of the village. They didn't pay him much and so he always remained poor.

Hema came out into the cold rainy night to offer his tiny hut to the Guru and his friends. 'It's not much better than staying outside,' he said, 'but you're very welcome to come and share it with me if you want.'

The Guru was delighted to accept and Hema took them to his home. Here he cooked them the best food he had, which was not very much, but Arjan ate it as if it was food for a king. And when they settled down on the floor to sleep Hema gave the Guru his only blanket to cover himself.

The Guru stayed for some time with Hema who was pleased and honoured to have him.

Arjan said, 'Fine clothes and posh houses are no good to anyone. You can be happy and contented with a poor hut and a rough blanket if you serve others and love God.'

Sometime after Arjan left the village of Khanpur and after the poor corn-grinder, Hema had died, the Emperor sent his troops out. For some reason the Emperor was angry with the people of Khanpur. The Emperor's soldiers marched into the village, killed all the rich people they found there and burned down their houses.

Guru Arjan made it very clear that money and riches mean absolutely nothing to God. What is important is what sort of person you are.

The person who lives in a ruined hut with all his
    clothes torn,
a person with no class or family or respect from
    anyone,

a person who wanders in the wilderness,
a person with no relations or friends,
this person is the king of the whole world
   if his heart is full of the love of God.

(*from the* Guru Granth Sahib)

Guru Hargobind

Gur Arjan's son Hargobind was born in 1595 CE, became Guru at the age of eleven in 1606 on his father's martyrdom and died in 1644. Hargobind was quite a new type of guru: he wore a turban in the style of the Emperor and a sword on either side, one symbolic of his spiritual power, the other symbolic of the way he protected his people from tyranny. He rode a fine horse and built up a troop of volunteer Sikhs for self-defence in the face of growing persecution from the Emperor Jehangir (ruled 1605-1627) and more aggressively from his son Shah Jehan (ruled 1627-1658). In the face of uneven odds the Guru maintained protection for the growing Sikh community through skirmishes and battles with the imperial troops. Hargobind instilled a heroic character into the religion which stills persists today.

Guru Hargobind and the broken statue

In India the Hindus have many festivals for their gods and goddesses. The temples are decorated with flowers, hymns are sung and parties and fairs are held. The festivals are times of great merry-making and enjoyment for Hindus.

    Up in the green hills of the Punjab in India stood the temple of the great goddess, Durga. Durga is a powerful goddess whose great skill as a warrior defeated a wicked demon and saved the gods. But as well as being mighty and strong she is beautiful and calm. In this temple was a magnificent statue of her. The statue was so wonderfully carved that you could feel the quiet power of the goddess Durga.

    The time of year came for the festival of Durga. Flowers were brought into the temple, food was prepared and Hindus came from miles around to join in the celebrations. A fair was set up with market stalls, games, food to buy, dancing and music and the whole area was crowded with people.

And Guru Hargobind came too with some of his Sikh followers. Guru Hargobind had come because wherever there were lots of people gathered he was able to preach his message. He taught people that it was no use expecting to be saved by singing certain hymns and saying certain prayers and going to certain temples. What really mattered was your love for the One God. All these other things were a waste of time if you didn't love God. Guru Hargobind did not think much of statues of gods either.

'A statue is just a lump of stone carved by a man. We cannot know what God is like so how can we make a statue of God. Praying to statues of gods is no good. God is in your heart. Show your love for God by working hard and helping other people,' said Hargobind.

The Guru preached to the people and his Sikhs sang hymns and the people joined in. More and more people left the temple to come and listen to the Guru until there was a great crowd listening to Hargobind and hardly anyone in the temple at all.

A man by the name of Bharu walked through the great gateway of Durga's temple. One or two people were coming and going and the priests were there lighting candles and burning sweet-smelling joss-sticks, singing hymns and playing cymbals. In front of Bharu was the statue of the goddess. Flowers hung around the statue's neck and offerings of gold and precious things had been placed before her. She looked down, powerful and beautiful. Bharu went up to the statue, took out a hammer that he had hidden and smashed her nose off.

Priests and people were amazed. But before they had chance to say anything Bharu was gone. He ran out off the temple and away. The priests and people followed shouting for him to be stopped. As Bharu ran past the crowds listening to Guru Hargobind a great burly Sikh caught hold of Bharu and held him until the priests caught up and explained what the man had done.

Pushing through the crowd to hear what had happened came one of the princes of the Punjab. With him were servants and soldiers. As soon as he heard that Bharu had broken the statue of Durga he ordered that he should be stoned to death there and then for his dreadful behaviour. The prince didn't even wait to hear what Bharu had to say. He had heard enough.

People round about began to pick up stones ready to join in, when the Guru came forward. 'It seems as if this man has done something awful,' he said, 'but we haven't heard his side of the story yet. Give him first a chance to speak.'

This was agreed and Bharu spoke up. 'I haven't done anything wrong,' he said.

'You haven't done anything wrong!' spluttered one of the priests. 'You have smashed the statue.'

'But I haven't hurt you. If I've done something to upset the statue, then it's up to the statue to punish me.'

'Don't be silly,' said the priest. 'How can the statue punish you when it can't speak or move?'

'Exactly,' said Bharu. 'And if the statue can't speak or move how can you say your prayers to it and sing hymns to it? How can you expect it to forgive you your sins and save your souls? The statue is only a lump of stone and there's nothing wrong with breaking a piece of stone.'

The priest said nothing. He couldn't think of anything to say. The prince stood there full of anger but he couldn't think how to answer either. Everyone began to laugh. The prince and the priests began to get angrier. Then Guru Hargobind stepped forward again. What would he say to calm things down? After all everyone knew what he thought about praying to statues.

'You all know what I think about worshipping statues,' he said. 'I don't believe you can make a statue of God. We humans don't know what God is like. He is too big, too wonderful. He has no shape or colour. He is everywhere and of all time. How can you make a statue of God.'

Everyone went quiet. The priest and the prince looked as though they were going to lose their tempers. The prince's soldiers stood ready with their hands on their swords and even Bharu hadn't realised how much trouble he was going to cause.

But Hargobind went on: 'I don't believe in worshipping statues but I do believe that you should have respect for other people's religions. These Hindus believe that their statue is holy and you should respect that. Breaking their statue is like breaking their hearts and a man's heart is where God is. Bharu, you have done a great wrong to these people. And you must pay for it. You must offer them your honest apology and repair the statue.'

Everyone agreed that this was a very wise decision. The priests and the prince, the Sikhs and the Hindus and even Bharu agreed. He did say he was sorry to the Hindus and he repaired the statue of Durga himself. There had been no trouble because Guru Hargobind had shown that you can respect people with whom you do not agree.

Guru Hargobind did not write any hymns of his own. Perhaps his life was too full of action. But he knew the hymns of the other gurus and the saints and he liked to use these to explain to people what he wanted to say. Many times he tried to show that, although there are many religions and many races of people, there is only One God whatever we call him.

When Emperor Jehangir asked Hargobind to explain the difference between Hindus and Muslims, the Guru used the words of one of Guru Arjan's hymns:

God, the Merciful One loves everyone.

God is invisible and above everything;

He alone is God great and infinite.

I bow to the One God, the Lord of the earth:

God who made everything is everywhere.
God has many names, but God is One.

(*from the* Guru Granth Sahib)

Guru Har Rai

Har Rai became guru in 1644 on the death of his grandfather, Guru Hargobind. He was a peace-loving man whose only pleasure in hunting was to bring the animals back for his zoo. There were no major military campaigns during his guruship although armed Sikhs were called on to defend themselves on a number of occasions. The oppression of the non-Muslims by the Mughal emperor, Aurangzeb grew more severe at this time and Har Rai spent his time peacefully consolidating existing Sikh communities and proselytising in areas of the Punjab where the imperial government would not feel themselves politically threatened. Born in 1630, Guru Har Rai died in 1661 although he was suffering from no apparent illness at the time. It is suspected that he may have been poisoned by his jealous brother who was in league with the Emperor.

*

Guru Har Rai and a poor woman's bread

There lived on the edge of the hunting forest a poor old woman who did spinning to earn her living. And not too far away there lived the seventh Guru of the Sikhs. The old woman had often longed to see Guru Har Rai but she had never had the chance.

One day she earned a small amount of money from her spinning and bought with it some flour. She took it back to her tiny house and mixed it and kneaded it and cooked it on her fire as best as she could. And then she took the small bread cakes that she had made and stood by the side of a track that led from the forest.

Deep in the great forest Guru Har Rai and his Sikh friends had been spending a day of sport, riding and hunting. Har Rai was tired and hungry and made his way along one of the tracks that led out of the forest. As he came out of the trees there stood by the side of the road a poor old woman. Har Rai jumped down from his horse: 'I see you've been waiting here for some time,' he said. 'Have you anything I could eat? After the day's sport I'm hungry and it will be late before I get back home.'

'I have only these small bread cakes,' answered the old woman offering them to him. Without stopping to wash his hands Guru Har Rai took the bread cakes from the old woman he had never seen before and ate them as if they were the finest food that a king could eat. When he had finished he thanked her many times for the excellent meal and then rode off to join the hunt.

When the hunting party came back to their own village that evening Har Rai told the Sikhs of the kindness of the old woman who had nothing herself but was prepared to offer the Guru her food. But some of the hunting party were disgusted. 'It might have been kind,' they said to each other, 'but the Guru should not be eating without washing his hands, and he should not be eating food from a strange old woman in the forest. You don't know how dirty it might be.'

The next day was to be a day of enjoyment and sport too. That morning while the Guru was getting ready some of the Sikhs had made sweet cakes. They had made them with the finest pure flour and everything that went into them was rich and expensive. Carefully they were wrapped and prayers said over them so that they might be pure.

Later in the day when the Guru was resting from the hunt his Sikhs brought out the sweet cakes and offered them to him. Guru Har Rai said that he did not want them.

'But you ate unclean food made by a dirty old woman in her poor little hut yesterday. We have made these sweet cakes with all the best ingredients, we have said prayers over them that they might be pure and we have brought them to you carefully wrapped. Why could you eat the old woman's food and not ours?'

'I ate the old woman's food because it was made for me with love. Your food was made with pride,' answered Har Rai. The Sikhs realised that he was right. They had made the food carefully and cleanly but they had not done it with love for the Guru. They had done it to show him how he ought to eat. They asked him to forgive them.

*

All the Sikh gurus taught that saying prayers and not meaning them, or going to holy places without understanding why, or doing religious things without loving God were all a waste of time whether you were a Hindu, a Muslim or even a Sikh. The most important thing is to love God and to think about Him in everything you do.

People put on their best clothes and go to all sorts
  of places looking for God:
But they forget to make their hearts clean.
They won't find God
and they won't find happiness.
You must try to be a saint in your own home
and do as the Gurus have taught you;
Be truthful, be loving, and do good things for others.
This is the only way that you will know the truth
and be given God's grace.

(*from* Guru Ram Das *in the* Guru Granth Sahib)

*

Guru Har Krishen

Har Krishen, the eighth Guru, was only six years old when his father, Har Rai died and he succeeded him in 1661 CE. Although so young his father had confidence in his understanding of the Sikh faith and in his ability that he had no qualms about appointing him as his successor. Times were difficult for the Sikhs: the Emperor, Aurangzeb pursued an aggressive policy towards non-Muslims and a constant threat hung over the head of the Guru and his Sikhs. Har Krishen deliberately avoided political confrontation with the government and moved with the utmost diplomacy in the highest circles while never denying the principles he represented as the Guru of the Sikhs. He was born in 1656 and died in 1664 after tending small-pox victims in Delhi at the age of eight. He is often referred to as 'the Boy Guru'.

*

Guru Har Krishen, the Boy Guru

Har Krishen's father was the leader of the Sikhs. He spent his time serving his people. He travelled around the Punjab in the north of India preaching, joining in hymn singing and leading the prayers. It was no easy job because Emperor

Aurangzeb did not like the Sikhs at all. Har Krishen's father had to be extremely careful.

When Har Krishen was only six years old his father died. He had not been at all ill and some people thought that the Emperor must have had him poisoned although no-one could be sure. Just before he died Har Krishen's father called him and told him that he was to be the new leader of the Sikh people — at only six years old!

But Har Krishen had listened to his father while he had been alive. He had listened to the other Sikhs who lived in their village and he knew what he must do. Guru Nanak, the first leader of the Sikhs, had told his followers to love God, to work hard and to help other people. That was what the new Boy Guru knew he must do.

But it was not long before orders came from Emperor Aurangzeb in Delhi that the young Guru must come and pay him a visit. Har Krishen knew that the Emperor was up to no good and so he refused to come. The Emperor ordered Raja Jai Singh to send a message to Har Krishen that the Sikhs who lived in Delhi wanted to see their new guru. This was certainly true and Har Krishen could not refuse to go and see his people. He sent the message back that he would come to Delhi to see Jai Singh and the Sikhs as long as he did not have to meet the Emperor. This was agreed.

The young Boy Guru set off for Delhi. And as the news spread that he was going to the Emperor's city, many Sikhs began to follow him. They were armed with swords and knives. They believed that Emperor Auragzeb could not be trusted and they were determined to protect their young Guru. Har Krishen told them to turn back, but they took no notice. Still they followed him. He ordered them to go back to their homes, but they were worried what might happen to him. Finally Guru Har Krishen drew a line in the sand of the road and said that anyone who crossed the line could no longer be called one of his Sikhs. He was the Guru and he could look after himself with God's help. He continued on with his mother and a few friends to the Emperor's city.

When he arrived at the palace of the Raja, Jai Singh, he was greeted with great rejoicing. The Sikhs of Delhi were delighted to see him. They all came to see him, and he was especially glad to welcome the poor and the old and the sick, for he loved the people that no-one else loved.

While he was staying at Jai Singh's palace Emperor Aurangzeb kept his word not to see the Boy Guru, but he did come in secret to see the Raja. He wanted Raja Jai Singh to test the young Guru in some way. The Raja was not very keen. He was a true Sikh himself and did not believe it was right to test his leader. The Emperor insisted and it was decided that Jai Singh should disguise his queen and hide her among the other ladies of the palace. One of her servants would dress up in the Queen's fine clothes and sit on the throne next to Raja Jai Singh. The Emperor believed that if this trick could fool Har Krishen, then he couldn't be the true Guru of the Sikhs.

Har Krishen was called into the throne room. There were people in expensive clothes everywhere. Even the servants were well-dressed. The Raja sat on his throne with the false queen sitting beside him. Har Krishen was called forward. But as he reached the thrones a puzzled look came over his face. Speaking to the servant dressed in the Queen's clothes he said: 'But you are not the Queen.'

Har Krishen looked around at the other ladies in the room, some with jewels and some without, some with beautiful silks and others with the clothes of royal servants. At the back of a crowd of servants he pointed to the Raja's own wife: 'This is the Queen of Jai Singh,' he said. And it was.

During the time that Har Krishen was staying in Delhi there came to the city the dreaded disease of small-pox. Small-pox is a disease that almost always killed and people who caught it died in pain. The disease spread around the crowded city very quickly, especially in the poor areas where the people were living very close together in dirty conditions. The rich people either left the city or kept their doors closed, and the people suffering from the dreadful disease died alone and without comfort.

But the Boy Guru spent the months of the small-pox plague travelling around the poor areas of Delhi bringing food and comfort and medicine to the people that nobody cared about. Most of them died, but Har Krishen tried to give them the hope of the love of God.

It was not long before Har Krishen caught the disease. His eyes grew sore and red and he found it hard to breathe; his skin burned and yet he felt cold; whichever way he lay he was uncomfortable; and his body was covered with nasty painful spots. But Har Krishen believed that God knew what He was doing and that He had a plan for his death as well as for his life; he never cried out in pain and he never complained.

As the boy came near to death many of the Sikhs were in tears, but Har Krishen comforted them saying, 'Gurus may die but the words that they have spoken will live on for ever.'

After this Guru Har Krishen had all of the hymns by the other Gurus sung to him. And during the hymn singing he died. He was eight years old.

*

Emperor Aurangzeb sent a message to young Har Krishen while the Boy Guru lay dying. He wanted to meet him and talk to him. But it had been an order from Har Krishen's father that he must have nothing to do with the Emperor, and so he refused. However, he did send him a letter. Here is part of it:

If the True God does not live in your heart,
What are good eating and fancy clothes?
What's the point of fruit or best butter, of
    sweet sugar or fine flour or meat?
What's the point of posh clothes?

What's the point of comfortable furniture to laze about on?
What's the point of an army, or slaves and
   servants, or palaces to live in?
Nothing lasts for ever except the True Name of God.

(*from the* Guru Granth Sahib)

*

Guru Tegh Bahadur

Tegh Bahadur was born in 1621 CE the youngest son of Guru Hargobind. He was uncle and great uncle to the seventh and eighth gurus, Har Rai and Har Krishen respectively. His life had been one of quiet meditation and, although he was very much in touch with Sikh affairs, he held no active prominent position until his nomination by the Boy Guru, Har Krishen in 1664. He then undertook tours around the Punjab in spite of the dangerous antagonism of the Mughal Emperor, Aurangzeb whose spasmodic destruction of non-Muslim places of worship and higher taxes for non-Muslims were making life extremely difficult for the very large non-Muslim majority within his empire. Guru Tegh Bahadur was arrested as he defended the right to be Hindu of a group of Kashmiris who were under threat of forcible conversion to Islam. Three of the Guru's friends were cruelly tortured to death before his eyes but he failed to back down and was decapitated in 1675.

*

Guru Tegh Bahadur, the True Guru

When the eighth Guru of the Sikhs died he did not give the name of the man who was to be the next guru. All he said was that the next guru would be found in the village of Bakala. Unfortunately he had many relations in the village of Bakala and twenty two of them decided that they would be the next guru.

    Meanwhile out at sea a merchant called Makhan Shah was bringing back a valuable cargo from foreign lands when his ship ran aground in the sands of a desert island. There was nothing the crew could do to move the ship and it looked as if they would all die of hunger where they were stuck. Makhan Shah was a Sikh and he prayed to God to save him and his crew if that was what God wished. After some time a strong wind began to blow and the ship began to move slowly off the sand. And then they were free. Out into deeper waters they sailed safely home to India.

When Makhan Shah was back on dry land he decided that he would give 101 gold coins to the Guru of the Sikhs to help the poor people. This would be a 'thank you' to God for saving the life of his crew and himself. Makhan Shah set out for Bakala where he had heard the Guru was.

But imagine how puzzled he must have been when he found that there were twenty two gurus at Bakala.

Makhan Shah decided that he would give a little to each of them and see if he could tell which was the true Guru.

He went to each one in turn and offered him two gold coins. The gurus were keen to get their hands on the money and told him that he must not give any of the others any gold because they were all cheats and swindlers and liars. Each guru he visited told Makhan Shah that he was the true guru because he was the holiest and the best. But their words did not sound true to Makhan Shah.

Finally Makhan Shah came to the house of Tegh Bahadur. Tegh Bahadur was a quiet man who was often to be found thinking or praying by himself. He was the uncle of the last Guru. He did not seem to be the sort of man who could lead the Sikhs at a dangerous time when the anger of the Emperor was against them. But Makhan Shah went into his house and offered him the two gold coins. It was Makhan Shah's last chance. He had been so disappointed in all the others. Was he to be disappointed yet again?

He held out the two gold coins to Tegh Bahadur who sat alone and quiet in his house. 'Only two gold coins?' said Tegh Bahadur. 'Didn't you promise to give me 101 gold coins? Where are the other ninety-nine?'

Mukhan Shah realised that Tegh Bahadur must be the new guru. He was so excited and pleased that he ran upstairs and stood on the flat roof of the Guru's house waving his scarf and shouting, 'I've found the true Guru! I've found the true Guru!'

The people of the village came out to see what all the fuss was about. They could tell by Makhan Shah's face that what he said was true and it was not long before the whole village and the whole of the Punjab were also calling Tegh Bahadur the true Guru.

And the twenty one other gurus? Nothing was heard of them again.

Tegh Bahadur did not stay a quiet man who liked to stay in his house praying alone. He became a great Sikh leader, protecting the weak and helping the poor. He died defending a group of Hindus who were being persecuted by the Emperor.

*

Guru Tegh Bahadur always put his trust in God, even up to the moment he was executed on the orders of the Emperor. He wrote many hymns in which he tells his Sikhs to do the same:

> God can save you from wickedness; He can stop you
>   being afraid; He is the Lord of the helpless.
> God is always with you.

> Remember God;
> He gave you a human body, your family, your money
>   and your house.

> God and no-one else gives all happiness;
> Remember Him and you will be saved.

(*from* Guru Tegh Bahadur's Slokas 6, 8, 9, *from the* Guru Granth Sahib)

*

Guru Gobind Singh

The tenth Guru was born in 1666 CE, took office in 1675 and died in 1708. It was he who instituted the Khalsa, the army of soldier-saints with their Five Ks-kesh (uncut hair), kangha (a comb), kirpan (a sword), kachha (undershorts), and kara (a bangle). These represent various aspects of the Sikh religion. He devised the Sikh baptism ceremony and had Singh and Kaur, 'lion' (an Indian military epithet) and 'prince' (demonstrating female equality) added to the surnames of Sikh men and women respectively. A large part of the modern image of Sikhism dates from Gobind Singh. Much of his guruship was spent in battle and he lost all his four young sons in hostilities. The Emperor, Aurangzeb seems to have softened his attitude to the Guru who was summoned to see him when the Emperor died. His son, Bahadur Shah, was on much better terms with the Sikhs and gave Guru Gobind Singh the title of 'Holy Man of India'. The Guru was assassinated by a man in the pay of a former imperial minister. After his death he had decreed that the guruship should be vested in the holy book which became known as the Guru Granth Sahib and remains to this day the living guru for Sikhs.

*

Guru Gobind Singh and the heroes of Chamkaur

Emperor Aurangzeb wanted to change the religion of all the peoples of his great empire to his own religion. If they would not agree they were put to death and their money and houses were taken by the Emperor. Guru Gobind Singh's father had died to protect a group of Hindus who were being bullied by the Emperor's soldiers. Now Gobind Singh realised that the Sikhs themselves would have to fight back to save their own religion from the Emperor.

A great army was sent against the Sikhs who lived in the town of Anandpur with their Guru. The small number of Sikhs were surrounded but Guru Gobind Singh refused to give in. Days and weeks and months went by and the Sikhs of Anandpur were starving. They were even eating the leaves off the trees. By now some of them were ready to give in, so when the Emperor's general sent a message of peace promising that the people of the town would be free to go, the Guru had a hard job convincing them to keep up the fight.

To show the Sikhs that the Emperor's word could not be trusted, he had five carts filled with rubbish and old clothes. The carts set off early the next morning and were immediately attacked by the Emperor's men who thought the Sikhs were moving their valuables. It was obvious that they would have attacked if any other Sikhs had tried to get away from Anandpur.

But months went by and the Sikhs became desperate for peace. At last the Emperor sent a Hindu and a Muslim who were both prepared to swear on their holy books that this time the Sikhs would be safe to leave. They said that the Emperor was really sorry about the attack on the five cartloads of rubbish and nothing like it would happen again.

Guru Gobind Singh had no choice. If he did not accept, his Sikhs and his own family would starve to death. Besides which, if the Emperor was willing to swear on his holy book, surely he would not be lying this time.

The people of Anandpur packed the few things they could and followed the Guru and his family out of the town. The Emperor's soldiers watched them pass but did not attack. The Sikhs travelled on in safety until they came to the River Sirsa and here they made a camp for the night.

Just before the sun went down the Sikhs said their evening prayers. And as it began to grow dark they all started getting ready to sleep for the night. Then noises of horses were heard, the rumbling of many hooves and the calling of men. The Emperor's army was on the march. Sikhs took their swords, their shields, their bows and arrows, whatever they could use to protect themselves. And then the enemy charged. It was a dreadful battle. The Emperor's army at last retreated, but there were very many Sikhs dead and wounded. As the Sikhs and their families began to cross the river there came another attack. A few brave Sikhs stayed behind while the rest escaped across the water. A few brave men gave their lives so that many could live.

On the other side they were fairly safe. They could more easily stop the enemy soldiers crossing the river and they could pause for rest. But where was the Guru's wife and his two youngest sons? Nowhere could they be found and the next morning the Guru and his two older sons had to leave with the rest of the Sikhs. They came to the village of Chamkaur.

News came that the Emperor's troops were not far behind. When the sun rose the next day the village was surrounded by row upon row upon row of the enemy soldiers.

The Sikhs knew that they did not stand a chance of winning but they were going to show these soldiers just how brave a Sikh could be. One by one the Sikhs volunteered to go out and fight alone against the Emperor's men. Each one fought as bravely as he could for as long as he could to the cheers of the Sikhs back in the village. But finally each would be killed. And another would take his place.

After some time Guru Gobind's eldest son came to him. Ajit Singh asked his father if he could go to fight. He was certain to be killed, but the Guru had to let him do what he knew he must. Ajit Singh charged out onto the battlefield. Although he was only fourteen he fought with as much bravery as the Sikhs who had gone before. Guru Gobind Singh could only watch as the enemy cut him down.

Jujhar Singh aged only twelve came next to his father. He too wanted to face the enemy in battle. He dressed as a Sikh soldier and a small sword was found for him. And onto the battlefield he charged. Bravely he fought and bravely he died.

The Sikhs who were left in the village of Chamkaur now ordered Guru Gobind Singh to escape in the darkness. They would die to keep the enemy from following him, but they felt that he must get away to keep the Sikh religion alive. Gobind Singh agreed, and later that night in the darkness he passed quietly right through the middle of the Emperor's army to freedom. He took with him the tale of many brave Sikhs and the story of his own young sons who had died for their religion. This gave courage to Sikhs everywhere when they remembered Ajit Singh and Jujhar Singh, the Heroes of Chamkaur.

One of the most terrible things in the world is war. It dismayed Guru Gobind Singh to see that Emperor Aurangzeb was sending out his troops to fight and kill in the name of his religion. Gobind Singh believed that we are all children of God, we should all worship Him honestly, and that we can all live in peace together whatever our religion.

Some people shave their heads and become monks;
others sit in meditation and prayers;
some call themselves Hindus; others Muslims;
there are Shia and Sunni Muslims.
And yet men and women belong to one race in the world.
God who created all things, and God the good,
God in his kindness, and God in his mercy

is One God.

Even in our mistakes we should not separate God.

Worship One God who is the same teacher for all men.

For all men have the same body;

All men have the same soul.

(*from* Akal Ustat 85:15 *by Guru Gobind Singh*)

*

Guru Gobind Singh and the heroes of Sirhind

The Emperor of India had sent his troops against Guru Gobind Singh and his band of Sikhs. Desperately they turned to fight, but they had all their belongings with them, the women and children and old folk had to be cared for and behind where their camp was flowed the River Sirsa. As the Emperor's soldiers came forward the sun began to set and it grew dark very quickly. Things were serious.

Some brave Sikhs volunteered to stay and fight while the Guru got everyone to safety across the river. Bravely they fought against the huge army and slowed them down enough to give the others a chance to escape. But they could not hold on for long. Horses and men pushed against them and they were killed one by one.

Then the Emperor's army charged killing everyone they could catch, men and women, young or old. It made no difference to them. Many, many Sikhs were killed as they tried to cross that river and there were hardly any safe on the other side who hadn't lost a father or mother, or a son or a daughter.

Guru Gobind Singh turned his men to face the enemy on the other bank of the river. They shot arrows and threw spears across and the Emperor's army was brought to a stop. They could not cross the river while the Guru was there.

As the sun rose the next day families began to come together again. But there were so many killed that many families would never be together again. Guru Gobind Singh could not find his wife (She had been lost in the darkness and was later taken to Delhi by a friend.) He had his two older sons with him, but he couldn't find his two younger sons, Fateh Singh and Zorawar Singh. They had been in the care of their grandmother, Mata Gujri, and she couldn't be found either. And sadly the Guru had to carry on without them.

But they were safe. Fateh and Zorawar, aged nine and seven, had helped their grandmother through the cold waters of the river in the darkness. But once on the other side people were rushing everywhere. Sikhs with weapons were coming back to fight, families were looking for relations, others were running away as fast as they could. Arrows and stones flew through the darkness. Screams were heard in the night on both sides of the river. Fear was everywhere.

Fateh and Zorawar began to lead their grandmother to safety when they heard someone calling them: 'Boys! Over here! I'll take you somewhere safe.' It was Gangu, an old servant of their father's.

'Thank goodness you've found us,' said Fateh. 'We couldn't see anyone we knew.'

Gangu took the boys and their grandmother to his own village, finding his way in the darkness. And they slept that night in Gangu's house.

After they had gone to sleep Gangu was sorting out the few things they had brought with them. He found a small box containing quite a lot of money and some valuable jewellery that belonged to the family. And though he had been a servant of the family for many years, he was tempted and he took it.

After her prayers the next morning Mata Gujri found her money missing and began to question Gangu about it. She asked if anything else had been stolen, and whether there were any servants who might have stolen it. Gangu was ashamed and frightened and he lost his temper. 'You ungrateful woman!' he shouted. 'You think I stole your money, don't you? Well, I'm sorry I rescued you from the battle.'

Mata Gujri tried to calm him down but there was nothing she could say. Gangu decided that he would have to silence Mata Gujri and the Guru's two sons, so he sent a message to the chief of the village that he had captured them and was ready to hand them over to the Emperor's men. Soon the soldiers arrived and the grandmother and the two boys were arrested. Gangu was given a large reward for capturing them.

Fateh and Zorawar, aged nine and seven were locked in the prison tower at Sirhind with their old grandmother. They were wearing the clothes they had on when they had been arrested and were given nothing warmer to spend the night in. It was winter and very cold. They slept as best as they could with no bed or blankets huddled together on the stone floor of their prison cell.

The next morning the two young boys were taken to the court and brought before the Governor of Sirhind. They were ordered by the guards to bow to the Governor. But they looked him straight in the eye and said bravely, 'Long live the Guru and long live the Sikhs!'

The Governor was furious. 'What is the meaning of this rudeness?' he said. 'Do you not know how to behave in a court?'

'I'm sorry if it upsets you,' said Fateh, 'but that is the way we Sikhs greet each other.'

'Have we been captured by the enemy?' asked Zorawar.

'No. I'm not your enemy,' answered the Governor. 'I am your friend. You probably know that your father has been killed.' (This was not true. Guru Gobind Singh had escaped from the Emperor's soldiers and was alive and safe.) 'You have no-one now, so I will look after you. I will find a royal princess for you to marry. You will be given money and land and rich things. You shall have a palace with servants, good food and expensive clothes. But you must give up your Sikh religion first.'

'We would sooner die than give up our Sikh religion,' said the boys together.
'Then die you will,' replied the Governor shortly.

The boys were led out in chains to a place where a wall was being built. As they were taken the Governor kept trying to persuade them to give up their religion. He would talk to them kindly and then in an angry voice, but it made no difference. The boys were chained to the wall, a metre apart and the builder was ordered to continue building the wall around them.

As the bricks rose upwards, past their legs and waists, the Governor gave them chance to change their minds, but the boys remembered how other Sikhs had died in the past and it gave them courage. The wall reached their shoulders. 'Will you give up your religion? Is it really worth dying for?' shouted the Governor. But for a reply the two young boys began to sing the Sikh morning prayer.

The builder was ordered to finish the wall. The bricks rose above their heads and the wall was closed in. Here the two boys, aged seven and nine, died a slow death.

Sometime later when the Guru's wife managed to find her husband again, he was surrounded by a huge crowd of Sikhs singing hymns and praising God. She looked around and could not see any of her sons. When the prayers had finished she said, 'I cannot see my sons anywhere. Can you tell me where they are?'

'Your sons died for my thousands of Sikhs. They have given their lives to save the Sikh religion. These Sikhs are now our sons and while they are alive, I shall not think our boys have died for nothing.'

*

By the grace of God Almighty the Sikh Brotherhood
   was formed.
All Sikhs are commanded to look upon the Holy Book
   as the Guru.
Anyone who wants to see the Guru must search for
   knowledge in the pages of the Holy Book.
People who are pure in their hearts will find the
   way they are looking for in its hymns.
The pure shall reign supreme; they shall be free.
The people who have left us will come back again
   and those who ask God for his protection
     shall be saved.

(The Sikh Congregational Prayer)

*

The Christians

Saint Matthew, Apostle and Evangelist

Matthew was one of the twelve apostles of Jesus and formerly a tax collector. Rome exacted tributes from its provinces which were divided into tax districts. Having no civil service the privilege of tax collection was farmed out to individuals or syndicates on the basis of rival bids. The tax collectors had then to collect the tax plus the Jewish religious tithe, recoup their bid paid to Rome and add on their own profit. They were regarded as selfish and evil and as traitors to their own people. Capernaum on the north-west coast of Lake Galilee, one of the first centres of Jesus's ministry, lay on the road from the port of Caesarea to Damascus, and also on the north-south road along the Jordan valley. It would therefore be a prime target for the tax collectors who charged duty on the transport and sale of goods.

Early Church tradition attributes the first book of the New Testament to Matthew though it is now thought that this is a compilation in Greek written about 80 CE, though based on an original Aramaic 'Sayings of Jesus' collected by Matthew.

*

Matthew the hated tax collector

Matthew sat in his tax office in the city of Capernaum in Galilee. A queue of people stood grumbling to each other as Matthew recorded their names and took their money. Matthew knew they weren't grumbling just because he was keeping them waiting, but because no-one liked the tax collectors. Galilee was ruled by the Romans who had no tax collectors of their own. The Romans sold the job of tax collector to whoever paid them most. After that the tax collector had to pay the Romans the taxes they demanded, but whatever else he could get from the people he could keep. No-one likes paying taxes anyway, but when people could see the tax collectors getting rich on their hard-earned money, they grew to hate them.

Outside in the street Matthew could hear the noise of a crowd coming nearer. He knew that a preacher called Jesus had been in the town for some time healing the sick and teaching people in the synagogues. 'Love your enemies and pray for the people who do you wrong,' Jesus said. 'Always treat other people as you'd want them to treat you.' But these weren't messages that Matthew wanted to hear.

The crowd was coming closer down the street, probably on their way down to the shore of the lake where Jesus would speak to them. Matthew laughed to himself and concentrated on the figures and the piles of coins in front of him, and so it was some time before he realised that everything had gone very quiet.

Matthew looked up and saw the crowd standing outside his office window and Jesus at the front of them looking in at him. Nothing was said for a few moments as Matthew felt Jesus's eyes on him, and then Jesus spoke: 'Matthew, follow me.' And to the amazement of everyone including Matthew himself, the greedy tax collector left his table and his piles of money and went with Jesus.

Later that day Jesus sat in Matthew's expensive and beautiful house eating the evening meal. Sitting at the table with him were many of Matthew's tax collector friends and other people who had made their money in unfair ways.

As Jesus left the house some of the religious Jews were waiting outside the gates. They said to his disciples, 'So your master preaches about being good, and yet he goes to eat with evil people like tax collectors!'

Jesus heard what they said, 'Healthy people don't need doctors, only the sick. I don't need to preach to good people, only to the wicked.'

Matthew's life changed completely. Instead of worrying about making as much money as he could, he spent his time travelling with Jesus or on his own teaching people about the love of God.

Jesus sent his disciples out to preach and told them, 'You don't need a wallet full of money or a case full of clothes, not even a walking stick for the road. The work you do will earn you enough to live on.'

*

Jesus said,
'Don't store up treasure for yourself on earth. It will go rusty or the moths will eat it or thieves will break in and steal it. Store up treasures in heaven where there are no moths and no rust, where no thieves can break in. Your heart is where your treasure is.

No-one can serve two masters: you'll either hate the first and love the second; or you will respect the first and think nothing of the second. You cannot be the slave of both God and of money.'

(*from* The Sermon on the Mount, St Matthew 6:19-21, 24)

*

Saint Philip the Deacon

Philip the Deacon is not thought to have been the same Philip who was one of Jesus's original twelve disciples. This Philip was appointed as one of seven Greek-speaking Christian Jews by the Twelve. Most Jews throughout the world spoke the contemporary lingua franca which was Greek and read the Bible in its Greek version, the Septuagint reputedly translated by seventy Jewish scholars in Alexandria (Egypt) during the 2nd and 1st centuries BCE. Tradition names the first non-Jewish convert to Christianity as Judich, treasurer to the Queen of Ethiopia and holds that he returned as a missionary to his people. The capital of the kingdom was at Meroe on the River Nile north of Khartoum in modern Sudan.

*

Philip baptises the first foreigner

Since the death of Jesus his disciples had travelled the land telling everyone the stories and sayings that he had taught them. They preached in the Jewish synagogues and at the Temple in Jerusalem and many Jews became Christians.

The disciples who spoke Aramarc, also chose seven Jews who spoke Greek to help them with their work. In those days Greek was a language understood by people in many different countries. One of the seven was Stephen who became the first Christian to die for his faith. Another was Philip.

After Stephen's death the priests of the Temple began hunting for the Christians to stop them preaching to the Jews. Many of them left Jerusalem and scattered all over the country. Philip went north to Samaria where he preached in the villages and towns. Many people believed his words and he baptised them into the Christian religion.

After he had great success in the north of the country he set out south from Jerusalem on the desert road to Egypt. He had not travelled far when he caught up with a beautifully decorated carriage pulled by two powerful horses and attended by several servants. Riding in the carriage was an African by the name of Judich. He was a member of the Queen of Ethiopia's government, the minister in charge of all the royal money and treasure.

Judich, the royal treasurer was reading a scroll of the Jewish bible. He had been to visit the Temple at Jerusalem and had brought back with him a copy of the Book of Isaiah. Philip came up to the carriage and said, 'Do you understand what you are reading?'

'I cannot understand it unless someone will explain it to me,' said Judich.

The Queen's minister invited Philip to get into the carriage beside him. Philip read out these words from the Book of the Prophet Isaiah:

'He is like a sheep led away to be slaughtered that never makes a sound.'

'I don't understand,' said Judich. 'Who is Isaiah talking about?'

'Christians believe that Isaiah is talking about Jesus,' answered Philip, and he went on to tell the African who Jesus was, about his teaching and how he had been put to death by the Romans. He told him how Jesus had risen from the dead and how he lives in the hearts of all people who believe in him.

And Judich did believe and asked Philip how he could become a Christian. They stopped the horses and got down from the carriage. There was a stream nearby where Philip baptised Judich into the Christian religion, and he became the first person to join the Christian faith who was not a Jew.

Philip went on to tell more people about Jesus while the Ethiopian took his new religion back home to Africa.

*

We had all wandered off like sheep,
and each of us went our own way.
God took on his shoulders
the sins of all of us.
He was treated cruelly, but he put up with it quietly
like a sheep led away to be slaughtered
that never makes a sound.
And now his pain is over;
he shall be happy.
For his suffering
he shall set people free from their sins.

(*from* The Book of Isaiah 53:6-7, 11)

*

The Prayer of Benediction

O Lord Jesus Christ,
Bless the winds of the sky, and the rains,
   and the fruits of the earth, and, if you wish it,
   let there be joy and happiness in the world.
Let there be peace in our country and with the
   priests of your church; give peace to each and
   every one of us and to all governments.
O Lord, give rest to all our fathers, brothers
   and sisters who have died.
And give comfort to anyone who is in trouble,

in prison, away from home or held captive in
any way; save them with your love and please
remember me, your sinful servant.
O Lord, save your people and bless them.
Care for them and given them life forever.
Amen

(*from the* Liturgy of the Ethiopian Orthodox Church)

*

Saint Thomas, Apostle of India

Saint Thomas, one of Jesus's twelve apostles, came to India about 52 CE and probably preached initially to the Jewish merchant communities in the cities of King Gudnaphar's Scytho-Indian Empire which included the Punjab. He also went south and founded churches in Kerala which still survive and whose adherents, followers of the Syrian Orthodox rite, call themselves St Thomas' Christians. St Thomas was speared to death, according to one tradition, at the orders of the Madrassi king and his remains are interred in the cathedral bearing his name at Mylapore just outside the city of Madras.

*

The legend of Saint Thomas's palace

Jesus had told his disciples that they must take his message and tell it to the people of all the world. Now here was Thomas in India many miles from home and wishing that he'd never come. Thomas walked the streets of the city of Takshasila in the Punjab where King Gudnaphar ruled his empire. Thomas needed work and asked if there was a job for a builder, for he could work with wood and stone.

Thomas was overheard by one of the King's men: 'You're a builder from Jerusalem? What luck! My master, King Gudnaphar wants a palace built as fine as the palace of King Solomon in Jerusalem. You're just the man we need.'

So Thomas was brought before the King. 'Tell me what you can do,' said Gudnaphar.

'In wood, your majesty, I can make ploughs, yokes, balances and pulleys, oars and masts and ships. In stone I can make pillars, temples and palaces.'

'You are indeed the man for the job,' said the delighted King.

Gudnaphar took his new builder to the place some miles from the city where his new palace was to be built. The land there was covered with trees and some of it was marshy. 'I shall want you to start right away and build me a palace as beautiful as the famous palace of King Solomon.'

'I can build you a palace, your majesty, but I won't be able to start until November. I shall have it finished by April, however.'

'That would be fast work indeed,' said the King, 'but you can't work through the winter. You must start now while the weather is good.'

'I'm afraid it's that or nothing,' said Thomas.

The King agreed and when he finally saw the plans of the palace Thomas drew for him he knew it would be a palace worth waiting for. As November drew near King Gudnaphar sent a very large sum of money to Thomas so that he could employ workers to begin clearing the trees and so that he could buy the very best woods and stone to build his wonderful palace.

But as soon as Thomas had the money he began to go round the poor villages nearby, giving the hungry money for food, giving the sick money for medicines; Thomas paid for houses for the homeless and he made sure that orphans, widows and old people were properly cared for.

As the months went by the money began to run out but there was no sign of any palace.

King Gudnaphar sent more money so that Thomas could buy gold for the walls, marble for the floors, silver for the lamps; and Thomas gave all of it to the poor people of the villages.

As April came to an end the King set out to see his new palace, built for him in record time by Thomas from Jerusalem. Gudnaphar could think of nothing else. You can imagine his shock when he stood at the place where his palace should have been. He could see the trees all still standing and the marshy ground, but he could see no sign of a palace.

He asked a passer-by if he had seen Thomas. The King would like a word with him. 'You mean Thomas who has given money to the poor and hungry, who has looked after the sick and found homes for the homeless. He eats nothing himself but bread and water and he travels from village to village telling people about Jesus.'

'That's all very well but I can see no sign of my palace.'

'But haven't you seen the happiness on the faces of the people hereabouts,' replied the man.

Thomas was soon found by the King's soldiers and brought before him. And when the King demanded to see his new palace, Thomas calmly answered, 'You will certainly see the palace I have built you. But it is not an earthly palace. It is a palace in people's hearts, a heavenly palace that you will not see in this life.'

King Gudnaphar was disappointed and angry. He ordered Thomas the builder to be dragged off to prison.

'You have made a fool of me and wasted my money,' said Gudnaphar. 'You will die a horrible death. Your skin will be stripped off piece by little piece, and then you will be burned alive.'

Thomas was taken away saying, 'I shall fear nothing, only believe in God.'

That very night Prince Gad, the brother of the King was suddenly taken seriously ill and in the early hours of the morning he died. His soul was taken to Heaven where the angels told him that he could choose a heavenly palace to live in. Prince Gad looked at all the beautiful buildings and soon noticed one that was more magnificent than all the rest. 'I should like to spend forever in a palace like that,' said Gad.

'That palace was built for your brother Gudnaphar by Thomas the builder who has cared for the poor with the King's money,' said the angels.

As King Gudnaphar lay sleeping his brother, Prince Gad appeared before him and told him of the wonderful palace that Thomas had built for him in Heaven. The King understood and leaped out of bed waking his guards with orders to set Thomas free immediately. From that day Gudnaphar gave his money generously to the poor and continued to build his palace in Heaven.

*

The Common Prayer

You are holy, O God.
You are holy, Almighty Lord
You are holy, Ever-living Lord.
You were born for us — have mercy on us.
Lord, have mercy on us.
Lord, be kind and merciful to us.
Lord, accept our worship and our prayers
  and have mercy on us.
Glory to You, O God.
Glory to You the Maker of Everything.
Glory to You, Christ the King,
You show loving-kindness to us your sinful servants.
Bless us, Lord.

(*from the* Kauma of the Malabar Jacobite Church)

*

Saint Peter the Apostle

Peter was the leader of the disciples after the death of Jesus (c 30 CE) and after missionary activity is believed to have taken his place as the first bishop (chief elder) of the Christian community in Rome. Roman Catholic Christians hold this position to be supreme in the Church. Peter is believed to have suffered martyrdom under the persecutions of the Roman Emperor Nero (37-68 CE). He is reputed to have been buried under the present high altar in St Peter's Cathedral and there is archaeological evidence to support this. The Gospel of St Mark in the New Testament is believed by some to be largely the testimony of Peter written down by Mark in Rome for the benefit of Christians there.

*

Peter, the Rock

Simon had been a fisherman until Jesus had called him to join his group of followers. Jesus gave him a new name, Peter, which means 'the Rock', and told him that he was the rock on which the Christian Church would be built.

There lived in the city of Caesarea a Roman centurion called Cornelius. He didn't worship the many Roman gods, but prayed to the One God as the Jews do. One afternoon Cornelius was in his room when he had a vision. An angel came and spoke to him: 'Cornelius, God knows that you are a good man. What you must now do is to send for a man called Peter who is staying in the town of Joppa at the house of Simon the tanner.' The vision disappeared leaving Cornelius terrified and excited. Immediately he sent for two of his servants and for a soldier he knew to be a religious man. He told them about his vision of an angel and straightaway sent them to Joppa to find Peter.

The next day in Joppa Peter also had a vision. As he was praying he saw a great sheet come down from the sky. On the sheet was every kind of animal you can think of. A voice said, 'Peter, eat whatever animals you like.' 'But, Lord,' said Peter, 'I have never eaten any animal that Jews are not allowed to eat.' The voice replied, 'It is not up to you to decide which of God's creatures you can or cannot eat.'

The vision left Peter very puzzled. But at that moment he heard a knocking at the door and voices asking if Peter was staying there. They were the messengers from Cornelius who told Peter of the vision that their master had seen.

They stayed the night and the next day Peter travelled with them to Caesarea. When Cornelius saw Peter coming he fell on his knees before him, but Peter said, 'Stand up, Cornelius. I am only a man.'

Cornelius told Peter of the angel he had seen and Peter told him of what he himself had seen and heard. 'You know, of course, Cornelius, that I am a Jew and that I should not eat with you or come to your house, because you are a foreigner. But I understand the truth now that God has shown to me. God has no favourites amongst peoples. God will accept anybody whether they are Jewish or foreign as long as they love God and live a good life.'

And when Peter had finished speaking, everyone there felt God's Holy Spirit come among them. Peter then baptised the Roman centurion Cornelius as a member of the Christian Church.

*

A legend tells of the death of Peter many years later in Rome. Peter had travelled around Palestine, Turkey, Greece and Italy preaching to Jews and to foreigners but came at last to Rome, the capital of the Empire. Here he continued to tell people about Jesus.

But on one warm night in the middle of July a fire broke out near the city centre. It spread through the shops and houses, through the temple and fine buildings. The fire swept throughout the city completely out of control. For six days and nights the fire burned and when it finally died out nearly three quarters of the houses in Rome were either badly damaged or destroyed altogether. Thousands of Romans, rich and poor alike, were homeless.

Stories began to spread round the city that the Emperor was to blame. Emperor Nero, people said, had been seen on the night the fire started, standing on the palace tower dressed up as an actor, playing his harp and singing! In fact Nero had been miles away from Rome at his country villa, but he knew how difficult it is to prevent people talking. Nero decided that someone else should take the blame and he chose the Christians. The Christians were members of a new religion and claimed that God had been born as a man called Jesus who had died and risen from the dead some thirty years before in Jerusalem. Nero began to round up Christians. Many were tortured and many were killed.

The wives of two important friends of Nero had recently become Christians. Albinus and Agrippa, the husbands plotted together to have Peter arrested and killed. But Albinus's wife overheard their plans and rushed to warn Peter so that he could escape. 'I cannot run away just because there is danger,' said Peter.

'If you escape you will be able to carry on telling people about Jesus,' said Albinus's wife, and the other Christians agreed. And so, reluctantly, Peter decided to leave. He said goodbye to his friends and set off alone for the gates of the city.

Peter had not walked very far out of the city of Rome when he recognised a man walking towards him. It was Jesus! 'Lord, where are you going?' asked Peter in amazement.

'Peter, I am going to Rome — to be crucified again.'

Peter turned to face the city and the vision vanished. He knew what it meant and what he must do. Briskly he walked back into the city to the house where he had just left his Christian friends. He told them that he must do what Jesus wanted. He told them that if he was arrested by the soldiers, they would have to carry on his work teaching Jesus's message.

It was not long before four soldiers barged their way into the house and dragged Peter away in chains. He was taken before a judge and found guilty of preaching against the Roman gods. The sentence was passed: Peter would be crucified.

As he was taken to the place of execution Peter asked if he could be crucified upside down. He felt that he was not good enough to die in the same way as Jesus. Peter was nailed to the cross and hung upside down while his Christian friends wept. He prayed to God and in great pain he died.

*

Peter's body was taken down and buried in Rome. Many years later Emperor Constantine built a church over the grave. A great cathedral now stands in the same place in Rome, the cathedral of St Peter.

*

At Pentecost when God's Holy Spirit came to the disciples, Peter went out into the streets to tell the people what had happened. He recited part of a poem written by the prophet Joel:

God said,
In days to come
I will pour out my Spirit for everyone.
Sons and daughters will speak my truth,
young men will see visions,
and old men will dream dreams.
In the days to come
I will pour out my Spirit for everyone,
even for slaves,
and they will all speak my truth.
I will show you wonders in the heavens above
and signs on the earth below.
The sun will be turned into darkness
and the moon will be the colour of blood
before that great day of the Lord comes.
And then everyone who calls on the name of the Lord
will be saved.

(*from the* Acts of the Apostles 2:17-21)

*

Saint Paul, Apostle to the Gentiles

Saul was born of Jewish parents in the Greek city of Tarsus in the Roman pro-vince of Cilicia (now on the south-west coast of modern Turkey). After studying in a Pharisaic school in Jerusalem he joined with the Temple priests in their persecu-tion of Jewish Christians. Saul experienced a vision of Jesus (c.35 CE) some five years after the latter's death and became not only a convert to Christianity but perhaps its most zealous missionary. He is known by his Roman name of Paul after his conversion. Paul is known to Christians of Toman and Greek traditions as the Apostle to the Gentiles (ie. the non-Jews) because of his efforts in preaching Christianity and founding churches across the Graeco-Roman world. His letters to various Christian communities are preserved in the New Testament and had a formative effect on Christian thinking from the earliest times. Traditionally Paul is said to have suffered martyrdom in Rome under the persecutions of Emperor Nero (c.67 CE).

*

Saul, a hater of Christians

Saul was a Jew and a member of a religious group called the Pharisees. As a Pharisee he believed that it was very important to keep the many ancient Jewish laws and he was very hard on people who didn't. He believed that one day God would send a great prince who would drive out the Romans and make Israel strong and famous again. He would be a king greater than David and wiser than Solomon. So when Saul heard that there was a group who claimed that this king had come, that he was the son of a poor village carpenter, that this God on earth had been crucified like a common criminal, Saul was disgusted. And these followers of the Christ weren't clever educated men like himself, but ignorant country people most of whom couldn't even read or write.

Not long after Jesus's death the Temple priests began to attack the small group of Christians in Jerusalem. Stephen was one of the first to suffer. He was tried before the priests' court. He was found guilty of swearing against God, and he was sentenced to death by stoning. Stephen was dragged to a place outside the walls of the city and the people began to hurl stones at him. One of the members of the court stood by and watched gladly. It was Saul the Pharisee who thought that Stephen was getting just what he deserved. As Stephen died he called out, 'Lord, forgive these people for the wicked thing they are doing.'

By now Saul had grown so angry about the Christians that he asked the High

Priest for special permission to travel to the city of Damascus some 250 km to the north of Jerusalem. There he would hunt down any Christians and bring them back to Jerusalem to be tried. Saul set off with a number of friends determined to stop this new religion from spreading any further.

After many days travelling they came near to Damascus. Suddenly Saul fell down on the ground shielding his eyes. He was blinded by a fierce light and he heard a voice saying, 'Saul, Saul, why are you hunting me down?'

Saul called out, 'Who are you?' and the voice answered, 'I am Jesus, the one you are hunting for.'

The light faded and Saul staggered back to his feet unable to see at all. His friends had to lead him the rest of the way to Damascus.

In Damascus Saul was looked after by Christians until his sight came back. When he was fit and well again Saul visited a Jewish synagogue. There were many Pharisees there who were keen to hear what Saul had to say about the Christians. They knew he had permission from the High Priest to capture them and take them back to Jerusalem.

Saul began to speak to the silent waiting crowd. 'I am Saul. You know I have special permission from our High Priest to search out any Christians and take them back to be tried. But I have seen Jesus. On the way to this city Jesus spoke to me. And I believe that he is God as the Christians say he is.' The people were amazed.

During the following days Saul visited the synagogues in Damascus and preached about Jesus. Some people joined the Christians but many of them, especially those among the Pharisees thought that Saul was stirring up trouble. And in one house in the city a small gang plotted to murder him. From now on all the gates into the city were watched as members of the gang waited for a chance to catch Saul on his own.

But some of the new Christians heard rumours of the plot and one night Saul was lowered over the city walls in a basket, so that he could escape to join the disciples in Jerusalem.

*

After Paul had talked with Peter, the leader of the disciples, it was agreed that Peter would concentrate on telling the Jews about Jesus, while Paul would preach to foreigners. Paul began to travel to the great cities where he would preach to the people. In nearly every city he was able to start up a small Christian church, although in many places he was shouted down or chased out or even flogged and stoned. But Paul carried on anyway.

Up until now Paul had travelled around Asia in the lands where Israel, Jordan, Lebanon, Syria and Turkey are now. But one night Paul dreamed that a Greek stood there calling Paul across to Europe and he took this to be a message from God.

Paul first went to the town of Philippi where there were many Greeks and Romans but very few Jews. However, as always, he went to the place where the Jews worshipped, to preach there. One of the people who was baptised a Christian was a cloth merchant, a woman called Lydia who offered Paul the use of her house as his headquarters in Philippi.

One day when Paul was on his way to pray he was stopped by a slave girl. Her owners made lots of money from her because it was believed that a spirit lived inside her and that she could tell fortunes. She cried out, 'This man is a servant of God and he will show you the way to be saved.' Every day then the slave girl did the same thing until Paul could put up with it no longer. He turned to the girl and ordered the spirit to leave her. Immediately the girl's mind was peaceful and she could no longer tell fortunes.

But the girl's owners were furious because they had lost their source of power. They had Paul arrested and taken to court for causing trouble. Crowds of people joined in and the judge ordered that Paul should be flogged and thrown into prison. The jailer was given strict orders to keep the prisoner well locked up, and so Paul was taken to the deepest cell and had his feet fastened in the stocks.

It was midnight and Paul was praying when the whole prison was rocked by a violent earthquake and the cell doors burst open. But Paul did not try to escape. The jailer rushed in believing that his special prisoner had escaped, he drew his sword to kill himself. But when he heard Paul's voice calm and strong in the darkness he realised that this was indeed a special prisoner.

In the morning Paul demanded an apology from the court because he was actually a Roman citizen and should not have been treated in this way. Full of shame and embarrassment the court did apologise and sent soldiers to escort him from the jail. Back to Lydia's house he went where he carried on preaching about Jesus.

*

As a Pharisee Paul would never have mixed with people who were not Jews. As a Christian he believed that the whole human race was one in Christ:

You are all sons of God because you believe in Jesus Christ. There is no difference between Jews and Greeks, between slaves and the free, or between men and women. You are all one in Jesus Christ.

(*from* Paul's Letter to the Galatians 3:26-28)

*

The following hymn was probably not written by Paul but by earlier Christians. It is quoted by Paul in his letter to the church in Philippi:

He was God,
but He didn't just stay in his Heaven as God.
He became as nothing,
He became like a slave,
living a human life.

Being human
He humbly suffered death —
death on a cross.
But God raised Him high
and gave Him the name above all names
— that everyone
in Heaven and on earth
should kneel
at the name of Jesus
— and that everyone should sing
that Jesus Christ is Lord,
to the glory of God the Father.

(*from* Paul's Letter to the Church in Philippi 2:6-11)

*

Saint Mark the Evangelist

Inferences can be made from the New Testament about John Mark and he is held by the Eastern Church to be the writer, at Peter's inspiration, of the oldest of the four gospels, which dated about 64 CE. He is held by the Coptic (ie. Egyptian) Church to have been a native of Cyrenaica, the western coastal region of modern Libya, at that time part of the Roman Empire. He returned from his travels to North Africa for the first time in perhaps 58 CE and was martyred in Alexandria 68 CE. The Coptic Church recognises St Mark as its founding patriarch.

*

Saint Mark and the Christians in africa

Mark was a Jew from Africa living in Jerusalem with his parents. They had lived a comfortable life in Cyrenaica, North Africa and Mark had been to a good school where he had learned to read and write and had learned to speak Latin, Greek and Hebrew. But their home and lands had been attacked by tribesmen from the desert and the family had moved to Jerusalem.

At the time Jesus came to Jerusalem Mark was a young man. Jesus had caused quite a stir and Mark remembered well the last meal that he had shared with his disciples because they had used the upstairs room of his parents' house. Mark had followed them to the orchard where Jesus had been arrested by the soldiers. Indeed he had nearly been caught himself and had run away.

After Jesus had been killed on the cross by the Romans and the priests of the Temple, the disciples had come to Mark's house several times and had been there together when God's Holy Spirit came to them. The Christians of Jerusalem carried on using the house after that, so perhaps it can be called the first Christian church.

Mark spent many years travelling and teaching people about Jesus. He went with his cousin Barnabas and with Paul and eventually ended up in Rome. Here he met the leader of Jesus's disciples, Peter, and became great friends with him. Peter had been a fisherman and had never learned to read or write. He could not speak Latin or Greek anything like as well as Mark and so he used Mark as his secretary. Peter began to realise tht he must write down everything he could remember about his time with Jesus. Peter himself was getting old and the time would soon be coming when there would be no-one left alive who had actually been with Jesus. So Peter and Mark together wrote the story of Jesus.

Peter was put to death as a Christian by Emperor Nero and it is probably about this time that Mark left the city to continue his travels. Mark had long wanted to go back to North Africa where he had grown up. He had travelled to many countries in the Roman world, seen many sights and met lots of people, but he had never been back to the land where he had been born.

Mark sailed first to the city of Alexandria at the mouth of the River Nile in Egypt. It was a very large city famous throughout the world for its beautiful buildings, its temples, libraries and universities. There were many Jewish people there but most of the people were worshippers of many gods. Mark knew he was going to have a hard time.

Mark left the ship and walked towards the gate of the city. He was just one person among hundreds rushing here and there — merchants taking goods to the harbour, travellers from foreign countries, people doing their shopping, farmers bringing food to market, slaves hurrying about their masters' business, and Mark with a message to preach.

As Mark came through the enormous city gates the strap on his sandal broke. Fortunately one of the shops nearby happened to be a shoe-mender's. Mark hopped across and sat down to wait while the shoe-mender sewed the strap back on. And as he sat Mark told the shoe-mender where he had come from and why he had come. He told him of Jesus and how he had seen him, of his death and coming to life again, of the disciples taking the story and the teaching of Jesus to all the world. The shoe-mender stopped sewing the leather strap to listen. He was fascinated by Mark's story. It was such a change to hear someone talking about being kind to other people instead of being selfish and greedy. By the time Mark left the shop with his sandal fixed the shoe-mender had become a follower of Jesus.

So it wasn't just Mark who was preaching to the people of Alexandria, but the shoe-mender and then his family and very soon his friends too. The story and the teaching spread through the city so quickly that the priests of the many gods began to get worried. Mark became a wanted man.

Leaving the new Christian Church in Alexandria in safe hands, Mark left the city to return to his own country at last. Cyrenaica was many days' travel along the coast through dry and unfriendly desert. But when Mark arrived he had the same success as he had had in Alexandria. In the large cities as well as in the smaller villages Mark found people who wanted to hear what he had to say. He was pleased to see the Christian Church growing in the land where he had been born.

Some years later Mark was invited back to Alexandria to join in the Easter services and celebrations. Easter was the time when Jesus was crucified and rose again from the dead. When Mark arrived in Alexandria he realised that preparations were also taking place for the festival of one of the Egyptian gods. It was the Feast of Serapis, the bull-god of the underworld and one of the most popular gods in Alexandria.

Easter that year happened to be on the very same day as the Feast of Serapis. And as Mark stood at the altar of the Christian church in Alexandria giving thanks to God for the life of Jesus, a mob of angry Egyptians, worshippers of Serapis, broke down the doors and wrecked the building. Mark was captured, a rope was tied round his neck and he was dragged by the rioters through the streets of the city.

Mark, with his body bruised and many bones broken, spent that night in the city jail.

Next day Mark was dragged through the streets and when the mob got him back to the prison it was found that he was dead. A pile of wood was heaped up in front of the prison where Mark's body was to be burned, but it began to rain. It poured so heavily that it was impossible to light the fire and the crowd went home meaning to continue the fun the next day.

But that night as the rain lashed down, a group of Christians took Mark's body and buried it secret underneath the altar of the church where he had been preaching.

There are still Christians in Egypt and North Africa today and they look on Saint Mark as the first leader of their Church.

*

Jesus said,
'You know that the rulers of the world lord it over their people and great men like to show you how important they are. You mustn't be like that.

Whichever of you wants to become great must be the servant of all the others, and whichever of you wants to be the first must be everybody's slave. For even I did not come to be served; I came to serve.'

(*from* the Gospel According to Saint Mark 10:42-45)

*

A Prayer for Peace

Let us pray for the peace of God's church which reaches from one end of the earth to the other. Give us peace from heaven as well as peaceful life. Look after the rulers of the world, the armies and governments who keep the peace. Fill them with your peace, O King of Peace, and please be with us. You have given us everything, so take us for yourself. We call your name and ask You to fill our lives with your Holy Spirit so that we may not be beaten by wickedness.

(*from* the Liturgy of the Eucharist of the Coptic Orthodox Church)

Saint John the Divine, Apostle and Evangelist

John one of the twelve apostles is believed to have been somewhat younger than Jesus and to have died at the beginning of the reign of the Roman Emperor Trajan (ruled 98-117 CE). John was originally a disciple of John the Baptist, but became a follower of Jesus and known as 'the disciple whom Jesus loved.' Present at the crucifixion of Jesus, John was given the care of Jesus's mother, Mary and legend has it that he took her to Ephesus (near Izmir in modern Turkey) where she died. John is reputed to have escaped death while in Rome and then to have been exiled to the small (then Roman now Greek) island of Patmos off the west coast of Turkey by Emperor Domitian (ruled 81-96 CE). Tradition says that it was here that he wrote The Revelation, though some attribute this to one of his circle. After the Roman Senate repealed Domitian's sentences John returned to Ephesus in 96 CE where he completed his gospel which was published some time after his death by his followers.

*

John and the robber chief

St John is often known as 'the disciple that Jesus loved.' He lived a long and sometimes very dangerous life, but even when he was over ninety years old he still took his job very seriously and travelled many miles visiting the Christian Churches.

Once, John set out from the city of Ephesus to visit the Christians who lived thereabouts. John would arrive at a town and spend the night at the house of the local priest. The next day he would tell the people stories of the years he had spent as one of Jesus's twelve disciples and then he would set off on his travels again.

John came to a large town where the people of one church told him about Giles, a teenager whose parents had died. He was a good-looking boy, strong and intelligent, but the Christians were worried that he might fall into bad ways if he didn't have someone to look after him. John took the lad with him to the bishop in charge of the town's churches.

'I want you to care for this young man,' John said to the bishop. 'Bring him up as a Christian and treat him as if he were your own son.'

The bishop welcomed Giles warmly and promised John that he would look after him. John went on his way.

The bishop was true to his word. Young Giles lived in the Bishop's own house and ate at table with him as if he were one of his own family. The bishop taught him all he knew about Jesus and the things that Christians believe. The people of the church were very proud of the handsome lad on the day the bishop baptised him as a full member of the Christian Church.

But from that day things began to go wrong. The bishop was a busy man and he didn't seem to have the same time as he used to, to watch over the young man. Giles often went off into the town on his own and there he met bad company, youths who drank more than they should, who gambled their money away, and who caused trouble wherever they went. And Giles became one of them.

One evening the gang went out for a meal. They ate and drank and had a good time. As it grew very late, Giles who was sleepy with the wine, suddenly realised that all his friends had slipped away one by one, and he had to pay the bill for the lot of them.

'I've spent everything I had on you lot,' said Giles angrily when he next met them. 'Now I've no money at all.'

'Where do you think we get our money, Giles,' said one of the gang. 'Steal some like we do.' So that night Giles and one or two of the gang broke into a house and robbed the owners of their money and jewellery.

Giles found it easy and it was certainly nice to have money whenever he wanted it. His crimes grew worse. Sometimes someone would get in his way and he and his friends would beat them up. Once they injured a man so badly that he died the next day. One night Giles and a few of his gang packed some things and left the town.

Before many months had passed the name of Giles was feared throughout the area. Giles and his gang would attack anyone on the roads, rich or poor, young or old. No-one was safe. The gang robbed travellers and were just as happy to murder them. Giles became known as a robber chief of great violence and cruelty.

Some years passed and John was on his travels once again. He came back to the town where he had left the bishop in charge of the young Giles. The bishop hung his head in shame and sorrow when John asked about Giles. 'I have failed in what you asked me to do,' he said. 'Giles has become known as the fiercest and most wicked of robber chiefs. He is feared by anyone who has to travel the roads hereabouts. He is a thief and a murderer because I did not look after him.'

And though John had travelled far and had only just arrived, he called for a horse and set out towards the robber chief's hide-out. It was of no use that the people shouted to him not to ride into such danger, for John would not listen.

John left the town behind and rode through farming country until he came to the hills. He was riding up a deserted track when out from behind the rocks appeared two fierce bandits. They threatened John with their evil-looking knives, but he said 'Before you kill me I should like to be taken to your leader. He is an old friend of mine.'

The two men laughed. 'I'm sure he'd be very pleased to meet you,' said one.

John was taken to the robbers' camp, a dirty rough place where the gang argued and fought with each other, where they gambled, and drank their stolen wine. John stood calmly between the two men holding him prisoner. At his age he felt he had nothing to fear from death. And when Giles the robber chief came out, John could hardly recognise him. He remembered Giles as a fine-looking young man with honest friendly eyes. This man's face was scarred by fighting and there was no friendship in his eyes now.

But Giles recognised John. His heart felt sick and he turned to run. 'Why do you run away from me?' asked John. 'I have no weapons.' John put out his hand and stopped Giles from going and then he held him. The wicked robber chief broke down and cried.

'Come back with me,' said John. The gang were amazed to see Giles throw down his sword and his dagger and quietly ride off with the old man.

John took Giles back to his church where he blessed him and forgave him for his wickedness. And Giles began to live his life again following the way that Jesus taught.

*

My friends,
let us love one another
for love comes from God
and everyone who loves belongs to God and knows God.

Anyone who doesn't love doesn't know God
for God is love.
My friends,
because God has loved us so much,
we should love one another.
No-one has ever seen God,
but if we love one another
God will live in us.

(*from* John's First Letter to the Churches 4:7-8, 11-12)

*

Saint Polycarp, Bishop of Smyrna

Polycarp (c 69-155) was for over fifty years Bishop of Smyrna (modern Izmir, Turkey), a seaport on the Aegean coast of Roman Asia Minor. He knew St John the Apostle who lived at Ephesus to the south of Smyrna and thus forms one of the very few links with the apostles of Jesus and the historical early Christian Church. Polycarp was executed during the reign of Emperor Antoninus Pius (138-161 CE) as a result of sporadic local mob violence rather than as the victim of official Roman religious policy. Polycarp, a little of whose writing survives, is known, with St Ignatius of Antioch and other writers of the first century CE, as one of the Apostolic Fathers.

*

Polycarp goes to the sports

Smyrna was a city in the eastern Roman Empire. Its Christian bishop, Polycarp was away visiting Rome when his churches were attacked. The Roman Emperor demanded once again that everyone in the Empire should worship him as a god. Most people didn't mind — after all, they worshipped many gods, so one more would make no difference. But the Christians did mind; Christians believe that

Jesus is God and many had died rather than worship the Emperor.

Twelve Christians from Smyrna were arrested. It was the day of the sports and they were taken into the Stadium to die. The crowd laughed and cheered as they were led out, and the hungry roars of the lions could be heard as they waited to be fed.

'All you have to do is to burn incense before the statue of the Emperor and admit that he is a god,' said the Chief of Police, 'and we will let you go.'

All the Christians refused and prayed to God to let them die quickly, except for a young man called Quintus who was so afraid when he heard the hungry beasts in their cages, that he gave in and was set free. Eleven Christians were left in the arena. Then the gates to the cages were opened and the lions were let out. The crowd were looking forward to the fun. Whenever runaway slaves or prisoners of war were thrown to the lions they would run around and the lions would chase them and the crowd really enjoyed it. But these Christians just fell on their knees and the lions killed them quickly as they prayed. The crowd was angry and disappointed.

After the sports had finished the spectators went home shouting and causing trouble. 'Where's the Christian bishop?' they called. 'Throw Polycarp to the lions!'

So when the bishop came back from Rome he found he was a wanted man. But Polycarp did not want to run away. He had to be taken by the Christians of Smyrna to a farm out in the country where he would be safe.

But the Chief of Police soon found out the hiding place. When the police broke in Polycarp was praying. He did not try to escape. The police were amazed when they saw the dangerous man they had been sent to arrest — Polycarp was eighty-six years old!

'It must be what God wants,' said Polycarp. 'Bring them something to eat while I finish saying my prayers.'

When the police had finished their supper and Polycarp had said his prayers they were sorry they had to take him prisoner. Nevertheless Polycarp was lifted onto a donkey and taken back to the city of Smyrna. As the little procession rode into the city the Chief of Police passed in his carriage. He stopped and invited Polycarp to ride with him.

'Why die in pain?' said the Police Chief. 'You can carry on your religion and die of old age. All you have to do is burn incense before the Emperor's statue and say that he is Lord.'

'I worship only God in Jesus,' answered Polycarp. 'I shall never worship the Emperor as a god.'

That night in his prison cell Polycarp prayed not that God would save his life, but that God would give him the strength and courage to die a brave death in the sports' stadium the next day.

Next afternoon the stadium was filling up with the people of Smyrna, hoping for an exciting show. Polycarp could hear the noise of the crowd, but above it all he heard the sounds of the sword fighters sharpening their weapons and the roaring of the hungry lions. The sports began. From inside his cell Polycarp could hear and imagine everything: the roars, the screams, the clashing of metal, the cheers, the boos, the laughter, the applause told him all he needed to know.

The sports were nearly over and still Polycarp had not been sent for. At last his prison door was flung open and he was led out. But not into the arena. Instead he was taken up many flights of steps and when he came out into the open it was into the special seats where the Governor of the city of Smyrna sat.

'Look out there, Polycarp,' said the Governor. 'You can see the terrible deaths that your Christians are suffering. Why do you want to die in pain. All you have to do is burn incense before the statue of the Emperor to show that he is a god of the Romans and I shall set you free.'

'But the Emperor is not a god,' answered Polycarp. 'I have served Jesus for eighty-six years and he has never done me any harm. How can I do wrong to him now.'

When the crowd realised what was going on they shouted for Polycarp to be thrown to the lions, but the Governor refused. 'The lions are fed and the sports are ended,' he cried.

But still the crowd shouted for Polycarp's death. 'Burn him! Burn him!' A stake was driven into the ground in the centre of the arena. Wood was piled around it and Polycarp was dragged down the rows of seats to be tied to the wooden post. Polycarp prayed as the fire was lit but the wood seemed not to burn.

It was some time before the fire really began to blaze, but at last the flames licked high into the evening sky. Though Polycarp's body was burned to ashes almost two thousand years ago, Christians have never forgotten him to this day.

*

Polycarp had met the apostle and evangelist, Saint John, who lived in Ephesus to the south of Smyrna. This is what St John wrote about the Christian Church in Smyrna where Polycarp was bishop:

> I know the troubles you have had and how poor you are — and yet you
> *are* rich. Take no notice of the dreadful things some people have been
> saying about you. And don't be frightened of the sufferings that are to
> come. Some of you will be thrown into prison and you will suffer cruelly.
> Even if you have to face death, stay faithful to God and he will give you a
> crown, the crown of life.

(*from* the Revelation of St John the Divine 2:8-10)

*

Ignatius, Bishop of Antioch (c 35-107 CE) was taken overland to Rome to face execution for his Christian beliefs. He was kept for a while at Smyrna where he met Polycarp and from where he wrote a number of letters to various churches.

Never stop praying for other people, for there is always the hope that you may help them find God. Give the chance to hear what you have to say or you can show them by the way you behave. When they are angry with you, be quiet and calm: answer their proud words by being humble; answer their swearing by praying; answer their wickedness by staying faithful to God; answer their bullying by your gentleness. Never be in a hurry to get your own back, but act in the proper way to show them we are all brothers and sisters.

(*from* the Letter of Ignatius to the Ephesians 10)

*

Bibliography

Buddhist Legends (Buddhaghosa's
  Dhammapada-Attha-Katha)
  trans E. W. Burlingame, Harvard
  Oriental Series vols 28-30, Harvard
  University Press, 1921.

The Dhammapada
  trans Thomas Byrom, Wildwood House,
  1976

The Dhammapada
  trans Juan Mascaro, Penguin, 1973

The Gospel of Buddha
  ed. Paul Carus, Alcove Press, 1974

The Hundred Thousand Songs of Milarepa
  (2 Vols)
  trans Garma C. C. Chang, University
  Books, New York, 1962

Buddhist Scriptures
  trans Edward Conze, Penguin, 1959

The Buddha and his Path to Self-
  Enlightenment
  Ronald Fussell, The Buddhist Society, 16
  Gordon Square, London WC1, 1955

Buddhism
  Christmas Humphries, Penguin, 1951

Tales and Teachings of the Buddha
  John Garrett Jones, Allen and Unwin,
  1979

Buddhism in a Nutshell
  Narada Thera, Buddhist Publication
  Society, Kandy, Sri Lanka, 1975

Some Sayings of the Buddha
  trans F. L. Woodward, Oxford, 1973

China — Lore, Legend and Lyrics
  Rode Rohan Barondes, Peter Owen, 1959

Chinese Mythology
  Anthony Christie, Paul Hamlyn, 1968

The Tao and Chinese Culture
  Da Liu, Shocken Books, New York, 1979

The Sacred Books of China — The Texts of
  Taoism
  trans James Legge
  vol. XL of The Sacred Books of the East
  ed. F. Max Muller, Motilal Banarsidass,
  Delhi, 1966

Myths of China and Japan
  Donald A. Mackenzie, Gresham 1930

Pears Encyclopaedia of Myths and Legends of
  the Orient
  Sheila Savill, Pelham Books, 1977

Chinese Religion — An Introduction
  Laurence G. Thompson, Dickenson
  Publishing, California, 1975

Monkey by Wu Cheng-en
  trans Arthur Waley, Allen and Unwin,
  1942

Chinese Poems
  trans Arthur Waley, Unwin, 1946

Ballads and Stories from Tun-Huang
  trans Arthur Waley, Allen and Unwin,
  1960

Facets of Taoism — Essays in Chinese
  Religion
  ed Holmes Welch an Anna Seidel, Yale
  University Press, 1979

Religion and Ritual in Chinese Society
  ed Arthur P. Wolf, Stanford University
  Press, California, 1974

Mahabharata
  retold by William Buck, University of
  California Press, 1973

One Man and his Dog
  Henry Lefever, Lutterworth, 1973

The Legend of Krishna
Nigel Frith, Abacus, 1975

Indian Tales and Legends
J. E. B. Gray, Oxford, 1961

Hindu Scriptures
ed Nicol MacNicol, Dent, 1938

Upanishads
ed T. M. P. Mahadevan, Compton Russell,
Salisbury, 1977

Hindu Myths
ed Wendy Doniger O'Flaherty, Penguin,
1975

*The Five Sons of King Pandu — The Story of
the Mahabharata*
Elizabeth Seeger, Dent, 1967

The Ramayana of Valmiki
trans Hari Prasad Shashtri, (3 volumes),
ShantiShadan, London, 1962

Kavitavali
Tulsi Das, trans F. R. Allchin, Allen and
Unwin, 1964

Hindu Scriptures
ed R. C. Zaehner, Dent, 1966

A Treasury of Jewish Quotations
ed Joseph L. Baron, Thomas Yoseloff,
1956

The World's Great Story
Joan Comay, Weidenfeld and Nicolson,
1978

Encyclopaedia Judaica
Keter, Jerusalem, 1972

The Twelve Caesars
G. Suetonius Tranquillus, trans Robert
Graves, Allen Lane, 1957

The World of the Midrash
S. M. Lehrman, Thomas Yoseloff/World
Jewish Congress, 1961

The Golden Age of Alexandria
John Marlowe, Gollancz, 1971

The Emperor in the Roman World
Fergus Millar, Duckworth, 1977

Jewish People, Jewish Thought
Robert M. Seltzer, Macmillan, 1970

*Great Jewish Personalities in Ancient and
Medieval Times*
ed Simon Novek, Peter Own/B'nai B'rith

*Service of the Heart — Weekly Sabbath and
Festival Prayers for Home and Synagogue*
Union of Liberal and Progressive
Synagogues, 1967

Heroes of Islam
Series ed John Field, Islamic Information
Service, 1978

The Life and Ties of Muhammad
John Bagot Glubb, Hodder and Stoughton,
1970

*The Muslim Guide for Teachers, Employers,
Community Workers and Social
Administrators in Britain*
Mustafa Yusuf McDermott and Muhammad
Manazir Ahsan, The Islamic Foundation,
1980

Muslim Children's Library
ed Khurram Murad and Arshad Gamiel,
The Islamic Foundation, 1981

*The Meaning of the Glorious Qu'ran — Test
and Explanatory Translation*
trans Maramaduke Pickthall, Taj, Karachi

Islam — Beliefs and Teachings
Ghulam Sarwar, Muslim Educational Trust,
1980

Caravan of Dreams
Idries Shah, Octagon, 1968

Hazrat Abu Bakr
Nawab Sadr Yar Jung Bahadur Maulvi
Muhammad Habibur Rahman Khan
Sherwani, trans Syed Moinul Haq, Sh.
Muhammad Ashraf, Lahore, 1947

Islam for Children
Ahmad von Denffer, trans Hatifah von
Denffer, The Islamic Foundation, 1981

The Muslim Mind
Charis Waddy, Longman, 1976

Muhammad at Mecca
W. Montgomery Watt, Oxford University
Press, Karachi, 1953

The Sikhs
W. Owen Cole and Piara Singh Sambhi,
Routledge and Kegan Paul, 1978

*Pillars of Divine Philosophy – They Speak in
the Holy Granth*
author and Publ. Nasib Singh Dhillon,
London, 1976

History of the Sikh Gurus
Surjit Singh Gandhi, Gur Das Kapur,
Delhi, 1978

*The Sikh Religion – Its Gurus, Sacred
Writings and Authors (6 Volumes)*
Max Arthur Macauliffe, Oxford 1909

Guru Nanak and the Sikh Religion
W. H. McLeod, Oxford University Press,
Delhi, 1976

Guru Arjan Dev, the Apostle of Peace
G. S. Sidhu, Sikh Missionary Society,
1974

Guru Nanak (for children)
G. S. Sidhu, G. S. Sivia, Kirpal Singh Rai,
Sikh Missionary Society, 1969

The Guru's Way (for children)
G. S. Sidhu, G. S. Sivia, Kirpal Singh Rai,
Sikh Missionary Society, 1970

In the Guru's Footsteps
G. S. Sidhu, G. S. Sivia, Kirpal Singh Rai,
Sikh Missionary Society, 1971

The Saint-Soldier (Guru Gobind Singh)
G. S. Sidhu, G. S. Sivia, Kirpal Singh Rai,
Sikh Missionary Society, 1974

A History of the Sikhs, Vol. 2 1839-1974
Khushwant Singh, Oxford University Press,
Delhi, 1977

The Supreme Sacrifice of Guru Tegh Bahadur
Lakhinder Singh and Satinder Singh, Sikh
Missionary Society, 1975

A History of Eastern Christianity
Aziz S. Atiya, Methuen, 1968

Peter in the New Testament
ed Brown, Donfried and Reumann,
Chapman, 1973

The Indian Christians of St. Thomas
L. W. Brown, Cambridge, 1956

The Twelve Apostles
Ronald Brownrigg, Weidenfeld and
Nicolson, 1974

The Synoptic Gospels
D. B. J. Campbell, John Murray, 1966

Peter – Disciple, Apostle, Martyr
Oscar Cullman, trans F. V. Filson, SCM
Press, 1953

Eastern Christian Liturgies
Peter D. Day, Irish University Press,
Shannon, 1972

*The Fathers of the Church Vol. 19 –
Eusebius Pamphili Ecclesiastical History
1-5*
ed. Roy J. Deferrari, Fathers of the
Church, 1953

The First Advance Church History Vol. 1
John Foster, SPCK, 1972

The Life of Christ
H. A. Guy, Macmillan, 1969

The Apocryphal New Testament
ed and trans Montague Rhodes James,
Oxford, 1924

All the Apostles of the Bible
Herbert Lockyer, Pickering and Inglis,
1972

A History of Christianity in India
George Mark Moraes, Manaktalas,
Bombay, 1964

Traditions of the St. Thomas Christians
A. Mathias Mundadan, Dharmaram
College, Bangalore, 1970

New Testament Apocrypha (2 Vols)
ed W. Schneemelcher, Lutterworth, 1967

The Fathers of the Church Vol. 1 — The
  Apostolic Fathers
  ed Ludwig Schopp, CIMA Publishing,
  New York, 1947

A New Eusebius
  ed. J. Stevenson, SPCK, 1957

The Bones of St Peter
  John Evangelist Walsh, Gallancz, 1983

NOTES

NOTES

NOTES

NOTES

NOTES